Gerontographics

Gerontographics

Life-Stage Segmentation for
Marketing Strategy Development

GEORGE P. MOSCHIS

QUORUM BOOKS
Westport, Connecticut • London

Library of Congress Cataloging-in-Publication Data

Moschis, George P.
  Gerontographics : life-stage segmentation for marketing strategy
development / George P. Moschis.
      p.   cm.
  Includes bibliographical references and index.
  ISBN 1–56720–062–1 (alk. paper)
    1. Marketing—United States—Management. 2. Aged consumers—
United States. 3. Market segmentation—United States. I. Title.
  HF5415.13.M676 1996
  658.8'348—dc20   95–51412

British Library Cataloguing in Publication Data is available.

Library of Congress Catalog Card Number: 95–51412
ISBN: 1–56720–062–1

First published in 1996

Quorum Books, 88 Post Road West, Westport, CT 06881
An imprint of Greenwood Publishing Group, Inc.

Printed in the United States of America

The paper used in this book complies with the
Permanent Paper Standard issued by the National
Information Standards Organization (Z39.48–1984).

10   9   8   7   6   5   4   3   2   1

To Nancy

Contents

Figures and Tables

FIGURES

TABLES

Preface

"Gerontographics" is a life-stage model that was developed to help marketers better understand the heterogeneous older consumer market. The main purpose for building the Life-Stage model was to set forth a comprehensive conceptual framework that would describe, explain, and predict patterns of older consumer behavior. While this task appeared to be an ambitious effort, these requirements for a model of older consumer behavior had to be viable goals in order to offer decision makers a tool more useful than existing models.

The Life-Stage model is unique and different from other models of older consumer behavior in several ways. First, it is *built on state-of-the-art knowledge* from various disciplines; rather than relying on any single approach to, or assumption about, human behavior (such as demographics and personality), the model takes into account a wide variety of factors that can help explain various types of consumer behavior in later life. Second, the model was developed, tested, and validated *using multiple methods*; it is not only the result of empirical methods, but also reflects current thinking among consumer researchers as to how to study behavior. Third, because the marketplace is dynamic, the Life-Stage model is *flexible* to accommodate changes over time to reflect changes in the environment and in people, and the succession of new types (cohorts) of consumers, such as "baby boomers." Key variables that reflect these changes can be added and others can be deleted to *reflect the dynamics of the marketplace* and the factors responsible for older consumer behavior. Finally, the model is directly *linked to marketing strategies*; it suggests the specific courses of marketing action an organization should take for better results.

The approach used in constructing this model consisted of several steps. First, a large amount of information from several disciplines of social science was reviewed, analyzed, and synthesized. This information was necessary in order to develop a "state-of-the-art" understanding of scientific knowledge about human behavior, especially as it relates to older people. Second, the key concepts and theories were identified as viable components of a model of human behavior based on emerging theories and trends in various scientific fields, as well as supportive research in the consumer field. Thus, each specific concept or theory reviewed was used only to the extent that (1) it represented current thinking and consensus among researchers in other disciplines, and that (2) available consumer research data could either support, or be interpreted in the context of, these interdisciplinary contributions. Third, these ideas or potential components of a model were further screened based on their relevance to marketers and policy makers. That is, we sought to include concepts that would directly explain those aspects of older consumer behavior which would have implications for strategy development. For example, our interest was not in understanding how or why people age (aging processes), but rather in understanding the effects of aging on consumer behavior and the implications for practitioners. Fourth, the factors retained were used as input into a comprehensive model and, using sophisticated statistical methods, life stages were identified. The number of life stages in later life were based on qualitative and quantitative theory-driven research data.

Because our interest was not in presenting just another model, we took steps to validate the usefulness of the derived model and demonstrate its usefulness to marketers. We had to demonstrate that our model was *better* than existing models used by practitioners. In order to accomplish this, we reviewed existing models of consumer behavior used in marketing, evaluated these models in the context of the information representing state-of-the-art knowledge in other disciplines as well as research in the consumer field, and compared the most popular (existing) models with the Life-Stage model. This comparison was made on the basis of consumer behaviors and criteria which are *directly linked to marketing strategy*. In doing so, we can give decision makers a tool that can help in predicting the viability of marketing actions based on older consumer responses to the marketing variables of an organization. Finally, we demonstrated potential areas of marketing application of our model, and showed how its value can be enhanced by integrating the model with existing commercial databases.

The process of developing this model lasted nearly ten years and represents the efforts of several individuals who worked on this project in various capacities over time. It also incorporates the inputs of hundreds of practitioners who were informally interviewed about their decision-making needs when marketing to older consumers. We began building the bases for this model in the late 1970s, when our first databases on older consumers were first constructed and the available literature were compiled and analyzed. This exploratory stage lasted through the mid-1980s, and much of the credit for these earlier efforts is attributed to Dr. Ruth B. Smith (University of Baltimore) and Dr. Roy L. Moore (University of Kentucky), who at that time were affiliated with Georgia State University. The media coverage of the aging marketplace which began in the early 1980s created corporate awareness and demand for consulting services, providing us with opportunities to work with various organizations and obtain useful input on their marketing needs. Although the work we did for various organizations was not aimed at developing segments of older consumers, the data from more than a dozen focus groups suggested the preliminary typology of the life stages of older Americans.

The establishment of the Center for Mature Consumer Studies (CMCS) in 1987 created a vehicle for conducting empirical research and fully developing the Life-Stage model. Dr. Michael Mescon, former Dean of the College of Business Administration, and Dr. Barbara Payne, former Director of Georgia State University's Gerontology Center, were instrumental in making the establishment of a second "aging" center within the same university possible. GSU's Gerontology Center provided opportunities for faculty and doctoral students affiliated with CMCS to interact with colleagues from other disciplines, attend lectures given by distinguished scholars in the field of aging, and conduct research. The author is especially indebted to Dr. Payne for allowing him to work with her, do postdoctoral work in gerontology, and serve on the gerontology program faculty for several years.

Several hundred organizations provided input that was used in developing a model useful for practitioners. Through informal interviews over several years, much information was obtained from these individuals which helped shape the criteria used in assessing the efficacy of the Life-Stage model and in comparing the model to those models most frequently used by various organizations. The preliminary development and testing was greatly facilitated by a number of research studies that were funded by the American Association of Retired Persons' (AARP) Andrus Foundation and other government and corporate sponsors. The conceptual foundations of the Life-Stage model were refined in the late 1980s as a result of a United States Department of Agriculture–funded project, which provided opportunities for a thorough review of the literature on aging.

The conceptual and empirical work related to the Life-Stage model benefited a great deal from the work and assistance provided by several colleagues and former doctoral students over the years. Many of our former students, especially Dr. Ruth B. Smith, were instrumental in compiling published studies for earlier reviews, including "Consumer Socialization" (American Marketing Association's publication *Review in Marketing*, 1981) and *Consumer Socialization: A Life-Cycle Perspective* (Lexington Books, 1987). The conceptual foundations of the model also benefited from reviews by doctoral students in connection with doctoral student dissertations, especially from the work of Dr. Rose Johnson (Temple University) on information processing, Dr. Euehun Lee (Georgia State University) on event-history analysis, Dr. Karen Gibler (Mercer University) on senior housing, and Dr. Anil Mathur (Hofstra University) on caregiving. Dr. Mathur was also responsible for much of the data analysis applicable to the Life-Stage model. Other former students made various types of contributions. Dr. Pradeep Korgaonkar (Florida Atlantic University) provided encouragement and support at the initial stages of the first empirical study. Dr. Harash Sachdev

(Eastern Michigan University) provided major assistance with our second study. Also, the assistance provided by Dr. Euehun Lee is greatly appreciated. Dr. James Kellaris (University of Cincinnati) helped name the life stages of our model. Many of our colleagues in other universities offered useful suggestions. We are especially thankful to Dr. Ron Faber (University of Minnesota) for his constructive criticisms on earlier drafts of the conceptual portion of the model. We cannot name the dozens of other doctoral and graduate students who assisted us with our empirical studies collected through CMCS over the years, but their work is greatly appreciated. Early drafts of the materials in this book were prepared for class distribution in the author's graduate class, Marketing to Older Adults. I thank Dorothy Stoudemire and Annie Jordan for their assistance with typing, and Cassandra Parris for helping with proofing.

Gerontographics

CHAPTER 1

Introduction

The subject of "aging" has recently received a great deal of attention in the media and in our national dialogue due to the increasing size of the older population. Two factors have contributed to the increasing attention. First, a revolution in longevity is taking place in this country and around the world, as more people are living far longer lives than has ever been true in the history of mankind. For example, three-fourths of the people who are born today are expected to live to age 65, and half of them will live to the age of 80.

A second factor responsible for the increasing attention on aging has been the increase in birth rates in this country between 1946 and 1964. Those born between these years, the "baby boomers," increased our total population by half within a very short period of time. With the baby boomers approaching retirement years, the increasing size of the aging population has contributed to ongoing public debates regarding age-related issues in both government and media forums. Today, one cannot turn on the television or pick up a magazine or newspaper without noticing something about aging issues. Such concerns include long-term care, Medicare, health insurance for retirees, intergenerational equity, retirement policy, and Social Security, as well as topics concerning the maintenance of health through exercise and nutrition, and the changing occupations and lifestyles of older people.

The growth in the aging population is likely to affect businesses in a number of ways. First, companies will have to understand the consumption needs of older people and how the older market responds to various marketing activities of the firm. Businesses have already begun to respond to the needs of the aged population by developing new products or modifying existing ones. The increasing number of older adults puts more economic power in the hands of these consumers, who are likely to demand products and services suitable to their needs and lifestyles. Second, businesses are likely to be influenced by the aging workforce, which has implications for employee benefits, job training, job discrimination, eldercare programs, and pension design. Firms have already begun to realize that keeping an older person on the job may be more desirable than it has been in the past. Finding and training younger workers might not only become increasingly difficult, but businesses also would have to pay benefits to retired workers for a longer time. Finally, as the population ages, many younger workers must provide care for older family members, and companies are beginning to feel the pinch of eldercare benefits and employee absenteeism.

THE MATURE CONSUMER MARKET

There appears to be no consensus on the characteristics that define one as an "older person." Age per se is not a very good criterion to use because there is a great deal of variability in aging. Because aging is multidimensional, that is, people gradually grow old biologically, psychologically, and socially, any age boundary used is not likely to produce a meaningful definition. Simply put, people do not always look their age or act their age. It often becomes necessary to use an arbitrary age, and even chronological definitions need to be placed in a proper perspective. For example, marketers of nursing homes may use a higher age boundary than marketers of travel and leisure services. Yet, for practical purposes, we often use a lower age limit, usually 50 or 55, to include people who may have a need for a wide variety of products and services.

One common mistake marketers often make in developing strategy is believed to be the use of stereotypic profiles of older persons. For example, common stereotypes of older Americans include poor health, social isolation, and lack of interest in romance and adventure. While many older adults may fit such profiles, the reality is that many others do not fit these descriptions. The older consumer market (often referred to as the "mature market") consists of older people who exhibit a great deal of variability with respect to the way they look, think, and act. Therefore, any generalizations about older people are likely to be inaccurate.

Size, Composition, and Projections

Presently, there are approximately 55 million people in the United States age 55 and older, and approximately 33 million age 65 and older. Worldwide, there are approximately 300 million people over the age of 65. In the United States, the older population is expected to double in about 35 years. It is estimated that by the year 2030 there will be 108 million people in the United States over the age of 55 (about one-third of the projected total population in the United States, compared with 22% today), and 68 million age 65 and older. Worldwide, the 65-plus population is expected to nearly double in 20 years as economic conditions improve and health care becomes available to developing nations (Moschis 1992).

In the United States, the older population is not equally distributed across all age brackets; rather, it is highly skewed toward the younger age bracket (55–64). The older market's age distribution in the next 50 years will be affected by two major forces: first, the increasing survival rates of older age brackets; and second, the aging of 76 million baby boomers who will begin swelling the ranks of the mature market at the turn of the century. As the baby boomers age, they will be influencing the age composition to the point where the oldest segment (75+) will contain nearly as many as the 55–64 segment, or about one-third of the people age 55 and over (Table 1.1).

Profile of Older Consumers

Before we begin examining the mature consumers' purchasing patterns, we need to understand the basic demographic and lifestyle characteristics of this market. Such information is important not only in helping us understand their behavior as consumers in the marketplace, but also in describing and targeting certain subsegments of the mature market. Sociodemographic characteristics, in particular, as well as other attributes that can be identified and measured, can help businesses locate and target mature audiences possessing certain characteristics or having needs for specific products. In this section we describe the mature consumer market in terms of selected demographic and socioeconomic characteristics.

Demographic Characteristics. The mature market—that is, people age 55 and older—can be described in terms of basic demographic factors, including sex composition, marital status, living arrangements, and socioeconomic characteristics. Description by means of these characteristics provides useful information for a basic profile of the mature market.

With respect to the age composition of the subsegments of the mature market, in 1990 nearly 22 million of the approximately 53 million people age 55 and over were between the ages of 55 and 64, and 18 million were aged 65 to 74. Ten million were between the ages 75 and 84, and three million were 85 and older. While the mature market is heavily skewed toward the younger age group, this age composition is likely to be altered in the future as life expectancy increases and cohorts move through the various age ranks. The Bureau of the Census estimates for the year 2050 suggest an almost uniform proportion of age distribution of the population across age subsegments of the 55–and-over market (Figure 1.1).

One of the unique characteristics of the mature market is the disproportionate gender representation, which becomes increasingly greater with age. Since life expectancy for women is about six to seven years greater than that for men, one is not surprised to see larger numbers of females with increasing age. For example, at age 75, women outnumber men by a ratio of two-to-one. Although most people age 55 and over are married, the number of widows/widowers and singles increases with age. The majority of men tend to stay married throughout their life span, but there are as many unmarried women as married at age 65.

Table 1.1
Growth of the Older Population

(Numbers in thousands)

Year	Total (all ages) Number	50–54 Number	50–54 Percent	55–64 Number	55–64 Percent	65–74 Number	65–74 Percent	75–84 Number	75–84 Percent	85+ Number	85+ Percent
1900	75,995	2,943	3.9	4,003	5.3	2,187	2.9	771	1.0	122	0.2
1910	91,972	3,901	4.2	5,054	5.5	2,793	3.0	989	1.1	167	0.2
1920	105,711	4,735	4.5	6,532	6.2	3,464	3.3	1,259	1.2	210	0.2
1930	122,775	5,976	4.9	8,397	6.8	4,721	3.8	1,641	1.3	272	0.2
1940	131,669	7,255	5.5	10,572	8.0	6,376	4.8	2,278	1.7	365	0.3
1950	150,216	8,175	5.4	13,173	8.8	8,404	5.6	3,275	2.2	577	0.4
1960	179,323	9,606	5.4	15,572	8.7	10,997	6.1	4,634	2.6	929	0.5

4

Year										
1970	203,212	11,104	5.5	18,590	9.1	12,435	6.1	6,119	3.0	1,511	0.7
1980	226,546	11,710	5.2	21,703	9.6	15,581	6.9	7,729	3.4	2,240	1.0
1990	249,657	11,422	4.6	21,051	8.4	18,035	7.2	10,349	4.1	3,313	1.3
2000	267,955	17,356	6.5	23,767	8.9	17,677	6.6	12,318	4.6	4,926	1.8
2010	283,238	21,424	7.6	34,848	12.3	30,218	10.7	12,326	4.4	6,551	2.3
2020	296,597	18,621	6.3	40,298	13.6	29,855	10.1	14,486	4.9	7,081	2.4
2030	304,807	17,307	5.7	34,025	11.2	34,535	11.3	21,434	7.0	8,612	2.8
2040	308,559	19,887	6.4	34,717	11.3	29,272	9.5	24,882	8.1	12,834	4.2
2050	309,488	18,439	6.0	37,327	12.1	30,114	9.7	21,263	6.9	16,034	5.2

Source: U.S. Bureau of the Census, *1980 Census of Population*, PC80–81. General Population Characteristics, tables 42 and 45; "Estimates of the Population of the United States by Age, Sex, and Race: 1980 to 1986," Current Population Reports, Series P-25, No. 1000; "Projections of the Population of the United States by Age, Sex, and Race: 1983 to 2080" (Middle Series Projections), Current Population Reports, Series P-25, No. 952. Washington, D.C.: U.S. Government Printing Office, 1984.

Figure 1.1
Population: 2050

Age

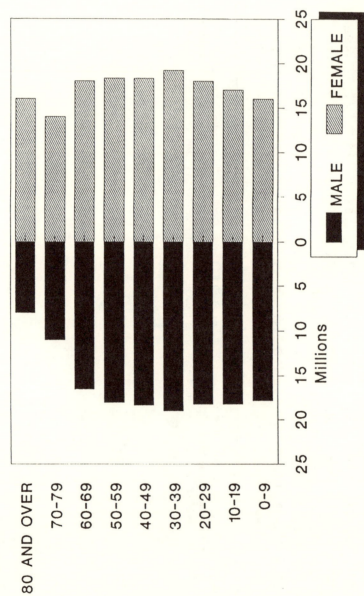

Source: U.S. Bureau of the Census; Cynthia M. Taeuber, "Age Structure of the U.S. Population in the 21st Century," paper presented at conference, "Tomorrow's Elderly: Planning for the Baby Boom Generation's Retirement," Americans for Generational Equity, Washington, D.C., April 1986. Projections based on Census Bureau's Middle Series," which assumes neither extreme decrease not extreme increase in current population trends.

Half of the women age 65 and over are widowed, since they are likely to outlive their spouses and marry spouses who are chronologically older.

While most Americans age 55 and over live with others, the percentage of those who live alone increases with age and varies by sex composition. At age 55, for example, 30% of all noninstitutionalized persons live alone, of whom 41% are women and only 16% are men. The trend during the last decade has been toward larger numbers of older people living alone.

The older population is heavily concentrated in certain regions of the country. Fewer than ten states account for half of the total U.S. population age 65 and older. This higher concentration is the result of both higher mobility to more desirable states by the elderly, and higher migration of the younger people to other states. Although the majority of older people live in urban areas, the city is not the preferred living area among older people. There has been an outflow of older people to suburbs over the last decades and this trend is likely to continue into the twenty-first century.

Socioeconomic Characteristics. The socioeconomic profile of older Americans varies depending on the type of criteria used to characterize or describe the financial well-being of the older person. Common characteristics include education, household income, discretionary income, and net worth. One distinctive characteristic of the older population is its relatively lower level of education. Only 11% of people age 65 and over have a college degree in comparison to younger people, especially those age 35 and under, who are more than three times as likely to have a college education. Illiteracy rates are higher among the very old and minority elderly. The older person's household income varies on the basis of their employment status. Household income is the highest immediately before retirement, usually between the ages of 55 and 65. Furthermore, with age, fewer people in the household are likely to be employed because older households are smaller. Thus, household income is not a very accurate predictor of the older person's financial well-being, and per capita household income is a more acceptable criterion because it adjusts for household size. An even better predictor than per capita household income is the older person's available income for spending on nonnecessity items—that is, discretionary income. This measure of financial well-being is probably more relevant to most marketers because it measures the older person's ability to spend. Per capita discretionary income is an even more accurate measure because it takes into account family size. On the basis of this criterion, older people (age 65 and over) have the greatest buying ability, followed by the bracket aged 55 to 64, both of which have a higher per capita discretionary income than younger age groups.

While household income and discretionary income are indicators of a person's ability to spend, many things on which younger people spend major portions of their money (e.g., mortgage, savings for retirement) older people may not have the need to purchase. Thus, it is also important to look at the older person's socioeconomic status from the standpoint of consumption needs and total assets accumulated over time in relation to his/her debts—that is, net worth. To illus-

trate the difference between household income and net worth as criteria of economic well-being, those age 65 and over have half of the household income of
those under age 35, while their net worth is ten times as high (six times as high,
if one excludes home equity) (Moschis 1992).

Health Status. There is a tendency among older adults to evaluate their health
favorably, since the body tends to adapt to its own frailties. However, reality is
that most older adults are not as healthy as they think they are. For example,
four in five people age 65 and over have at least one chronic condition, and
85% take medication. Although the prevalence of disease is high among older
adults, this does not keep them from living active lives. Only one in six older
Americans age 65 and over has a functional limitation that keeps him or her
from carrying out day-to-day activities.

Aging and Age-Related Changes

In the process of growing old, individuals undergo gradual changes that affect
the way they interact with their environment and respond to marketing efforts
of various organizations. The changes that occur with aging are biophysical as
well as psychosocial. The first type includes changes in sensory and intellectual
functioning of the individual, diminished mobility and strength, changes in outer
appearance, and the general aging and death of cells that affects all bodily
systems. These changes make a person less able to withstand environmental
pressures, contributing to one's greater susceptibility to disease. Psychosocial
aging, on the other hand, includes changes in the person's mental functioning,
personality, and the composite of social lifestyles that defines various social roles
people are expected to play at different stages in life (e.g., ''grandfather,'' ''retiree''). Understanding biophysical and psychosocial changes that arise from
growing old can help marketers better tailor products and services to the needs
of the aging population.

Biophysical changes in late life make it increasingly difficult for older persons
to master their environment. These changes may not necessarily interfere with
the older person's ability to function independently, but they may create stress
and frustration and require additional effort on the part of the older person to
function independently. To the extent that marketers of products and services
are aware of these changes, they can help older people compensate for their
frailties by making certain changes in their products and the methods of their
delivery.

The way consumers in general respond to marketing offerings depends on
how they perceive and interpret the information they receive from their environment, that is, the way they process information. In order to better understand
older consumers, one must examine consumer information-processing skills and
how these change in late life. With age, there are changes in the older consumer's ability to accurately perceive information via sensory systems; organize,
interpret, store, and retrieve information; and respond to external stimuli. It takes

longer for older adults than for their younger counterparts to process and use information. Although there may be several reasons for the increasing decline in information-processing speed and accuracy, much of the decline in infor- mation-processing abilities is attributed to biological factors, especially the de- cline in the efficiency of the central nervous system. Yet many other factors appear to affect this process. For example, information-processing efficiency is higher among those older individuals who have higher levels of education, pos- sess previous knowledge about and familiarity or experience with the task, and maintain an active lifestyle.

Some of the personality characteristics of older adults may also change in late life, and marketers must be aware of such changes. Motivations for consumption may differ from those of younger consumers. Messages should be designed accordingly, to reflect the psychological and motivational aspects of older con- sumers. Finally, a number of changes in social roles and social relationships occur in late life, and these changes call for different marketing strategies. For example, the husband's power as a decision maker in household purchases may decline as he retires and experiences declines in ability to function independ- ently, while the wife may take on roles once assumed by her husband. Simi- larly, older people may assume new roles as a result of their stage in life (e.g., ''retiree,'' ''grandparent'') and engage in behaviors consistent with these roles (e.g., buy products for grandchildren, use senior discounts and other products or services designed for retirees). Changes in such roles are often related to changes in relationships between the aging individuals and the various members in their immediate or distant environment. For example, retirement often con- tributes to the individual's contraction of certain social relationships (e.g., com- munication with younger employees) and the establishment of new relationships due to changes in lifestyles or status conferred by others (e.g., AARP member- ship).

Lifestyles of Older Adults

Activities, interests, attitudes, and values define one's lifestyles. Lifestyles of older people are affected by biophysical and psychosocial changes associated with advancing age. A number of activities intensify with age in late life. Use of mass media (especially newspapers and television) increases and so does gardening and landscaping. Older people like to participate in activities involv- ing social contact. With increasing age, older people may participate more in community and volunteering activities, entertain more at home, and shop more frequently accompanied by others. Also, with age, older people are becoming more involved in political issues and religious (spiritual) affairs. They may show increasing interest in a variety of games, depending on their physical capabilities and social opportunities. The increasing standard of living has recently enabled older persons to travel more domestically and internationally. As with many other age groups, greater awareness of the positive effects of exercise has contributed to the older person's increase in participation in a number of outdoor activities, especially walking. There is a wide variation in values and attitudes among the aged. Generally speaking, older adults are more likely than younger people to be conservative and have traditional values, and be satisfied with their lives; with age, they become increasingly introverted and resistant to change. Ageism still has a negative connotation as much among older people as it does among younger generations.

Marketers need to understand the lifestyles and values of the older population for several reasons. First, activities and interests of older people suggest needs for products and services. Second, activities, attitudes, and values are useful bases for segmenting the mature market and designing communication strategies that are congruent with their lifestyles. Finally, marketers must constantly monitor changes in values and lifestyles, and must try to understand differences in values held by successive generations in order to identify opportunities and more effectively adjust product offerings and communication strategies that appeal to these changes.

Consumption and Shopping Patterns

The older person's propensity to consume is affected by several factors, including the specific stage in life, early-life experiences, saving/spending attitudes, and preferences for spending on various types of products. With age, older people appear to be increasingly inclined to save more and spend less. This may reflect both decrease in consumption needs for major products and services (e.g., a house, college education for children) as well as an effort to better prepare oneself financially for late life. In addition, age differences in consumption among the young and the old may reflect the impact of different attitudes toward consumption formed as a result of different cohort experiences between those older individuals who experienced the Great Depression years and those (primarily baby boomers) who did not. Older people are more likely than younger adults to purchase specific products and services such as vacation homes, gardening and lawn care services, prescription and OTC drugs, money market funds and certificates of deposits, newspaper subscriptions, as well as a variety of products such as gifts for younger relatives (Moschis 1992).

Older consumers' shopping habits differ from those of younger consumers. Many older Americans who are socially isolated and have physical impairments often must use public transportation to get to the store. Proximity to various retail facilities is of great importance to older adults. For many older adults, shopping serves as an outlet for social interaction. Purchase frequency may decline for seasonal or nonessential items, but for essential items such as food, older people tend to shop as frequently as younger people. Furthermore, they tend to avoid shopping during evening hours, preferring morning hours instead (Moschis 1992).

Older people tend to be more "loyal" to stores than younger people, although this may reflect disloyalty on the part of younger adults due to higher mobility. However, older shoppers show strong patronage preferences for established types of stores, especially department stores. Reasons for patronizing specific outlets not only differ from reasons given by younger adults, but they also differ across types of stores or service providers. One important reason older people patronize various types of retail outlets is the personal relationship and the personnel's or staff's ability to help them with a variety of problems they may need assistance with. Older consumers normally have a smaller acceptable set of store choices in mind, and they may patronize any one of them due to reasons such as age-targeted incentives. For example, the effectiveness of money-saving incentives and senior discounts depends on the type of outlet or products/services purchased, and they are becoming important factors to the extent that quality and other important considerations (e.g., convenience) meet the older person's expectations.

Purchasing directly from the source is almost as common among older consumers as it is among their younger counterparts for certain types of products. Two major forces affect the older person's propensity to buy direct: (1) declining needs for several products in late life suppresses direct buying; and (2) the older person's inability to get to the store enhances direct buying options. The older person's propensity to buy direct depends on several factors such as type of product and select consumer characteristics. For example, products such as clothes and insurance policies can be effectively sold through direct mail; and older people who are retired and live in rural areas are more likely than their employed and urban counterparts to buy direct. Older people place a great deal of confidence in the direct marketer's name and reputation.

In purchasing products and services, consumers engage in various types of activities that include information seeking, product evaluation, and the purchase transaction. Older consumers are fairly similar to their younger counterparts with respect to the types of information they use, but they rely more on past experience and, in the absence of personal sources, they may rely more on information in the mass media. They are also more likely than younger consumers to look for information in the media, in part due to biophysical and psychosocial constraints associated with age (e.g., difficulty in getting to the store).

Older adults tend to have similar criteria as younger adults in evaluating products, but they may rely on different factors than their younger counterparts. For example, guarantees and similar risk-reducing cues are more important to older adults who tend to rely more on salespeople and informal sources of information (e.g., peers) as their ability to see, locate, and evaluate merchandise declines. However, the criteria used in evaluating products and services vary across different products and services (Moschis 1992).

Older consumers may be more brand-loyal than younger adults, but loyalty appears to be product-specific. While brand loyalty may reflect changes in lifestyles and needs, older adults are more likely to switch to other familiar brands when they are given incentives. With respect to their propensity to buy new products, studies show a wide variability across types of products and segments of older population. Older adults may buy new products and services that clearly communicate benefits to them such as convenience. However, another set of factors, such as mental health, education, and interest in products, is likely to affect their propensity to buy new products.

When purchasing products at a vendor's facility or at home, older consumers use similar methods of payment as their younger counterparts. Although older adults carry fewer credit cards, they use credit as often as younger consumers when buying goods and services. However, older people tend to use credit mainly for convenience purposes, while younger buyers tend to use it to finance consumption. This could explain the reason younger people carry a larger number of credit cards and are less likely to pay the entire monthly balance, since they have to spread debt over a larger number of credit cards.

Although older people are believed to be vulnerable to fraudulent activities and to be victims of high-pressure selling efforts, the available research does not show the extent to which these people are victimized and whether they are more vulnerable than younger people for certain types of products and services. Older people tend to report fewer bad buying experiences and higher levels of satisfaction with the products and services they buy than younger adults. This might be due to their lower level of awareness of unethical business practices, or due to their buying skills developed throughout life, which help them avoid purchasing situations likely to lead to bad experiences. Older consumers are more likely to be dissatisfied with purchases and consumption of products and services with which they have had little experience; and they tend to be less satisfied with products whose consumption requires the performance of various activities by the older person, activities likely to be affected by biophysical changes in late life. For such products and services, older consumers might attribute poor performance to the product or service provider, since they are likely to adapt to biophysical changes and may not be aware of their own frailties. Older consumers who are not satisfied with products and services may not always complain to the seller, but they may tell others of their unpleasant experiences or stop patronizing the company or service provider. The nature and the extent of their formal complaining depends on several factors such as economic and social consequences of their complaining behavior as well as their education level.

To summarize, the mature market differs from younger age groups. In addition, it is a very diverse market with respect to sociodemographic characteristics, lifestyles, attitudes, and consumption patterns. These differences are in part due to physical, psychological, and social changes that accompany aging. This diversity presents challenges and opportunities to marketers.

MARKET SEGMENTATION

Because of differences in attitudes, values, and behaviors among older consumers, a ''shotgun'' approach to marketing does not appear to be an effective strategy. A given marketing strategy may be effective with one category of older adults, while other groups of the mature market will find the same offerings less attractive. A more effective strategy to reach a heterogeneous market is to match company offerings with the needs of subgroups. Doing this calls for market segmentation and target marketing. Market segmentation refers to subdividing the market into several groupings, with each subsegment recognized for its preferences regarding products/services and methods of delivery. Target marketing refers to the development of a different viable marketing mix for each of the segments (Kotler 1984, p. 251).

Rationale for Segmentation

Segmentation analysis is based on the assumption that individuals differ in perceptions, attitudes, and consumption behavior, but these differences are not entirely idiosyncratic. That is, there should be subgroupings of the older population whose members share similarities, but differ markedly from members of other subgroupings.

Market segmentation appears to be an effective strategic tool for addressing the mature market, not only because this market is highly diversified but also because of its size. Older age groups are likely to be sizable as well, justifying the development of different strategies to reach them. Finally, segmentation provides opportunities for efficiency and specialization. Simply put, a company can achieve better results by designing marketing programs that match the needs of specific subsegments and by developing a market niche than by using the "shotgun" approach.

Bases for Segmentation

While segmentation analysis appears to be an easy concept to implement, it is surrounded by issues and controversies. There are presently numerous ways of subdividing the market, and no two ways are likely to produce similar results. For example, the mature market has been segmented into age groups such as 55–64, 65–74, and 75 or older (Lazer 1985). It has also been segmented according to lifestyles, such as VALS (Goldring & Company 1987; Gollub and Javitz 1989).

Because segmentation is based on the premise that subgroupings differ, any factor that shows variability in behavior in the marketplace can conceivably be used as a basis for developing subgroups. This wide choice poses a problem in selecting the optimal number and criteria that should be used. For example, is just one criterion such as age or lifestyle sufficient, or could better results be obtained by considering another criterion or several factors simultaneously? Which factor(s) should be used to segment the market, and why? How can marketers be sure they are using the best available segmentation tool?

PURPOSE

The purpose of this book is to present a model of market segmentation that is based on scientific evidence and compares favorably to other popular segmentation models. First, the book presents the rationale for the segmentation model based on a state-of-the-art review of relevant theories and research findings related to aging. Second, scientific evidence is used as a foundation for developing the segmentation model, describing its components, superior predictive power over existing models, and usefulness to marketing practitioners. Third, the book presents the results of two large-scale national studies to illustrate the value of the model in predicting the behavior of older Americans as consumers. These studies show how older consumers' responses to marketing offerings and communication variables (that is, components of marketing strategy) differ across segments, and how specific segments warrant the use of different strategies for greater marketing effectiveness. Finally, based on these data, the book outlines specific strategic and marketing tactics for targets of the older consumer market.

REFERENCES

Goldring & Company. (1987). *Geromarket Study*. Chicago: Goldring & Company.

Gollub, James, and Harold Javitz. (1989). "Six Ways to Age." *American Demographics*, 11 (June): 28–30, 35, 56.

Kotler, Philip. (1984). *Marketing Management* (5th ed.). Englewood Cliffs, NJ: Prentice-Hall.

Lazer, William. (1985). "Inside the Mature Market." *American Demographics* (March): 23–25, 48–49.

Moschis, George P. (1992). *Marketing to Older Consumers*. Westport, CT: Quorum Books.

CHAPTER 2

Theoretical Foundations of the Life-Stage Model

The segmentation model was built to explain consumer behavior in later life. Recognizing the diversity of the older population, the model had to be built on the premise that the mature consumer market is very heterogeneous; and understanding the consumer behavior of this market can best be accomplished by understanding the behavior of its subsegments. Thus, the primary focus in model building was to identify segments of older consumers that behave differently as well as the reasons for the observed differences in consumer behavior. Previous works (e.g., Moschis 1992; 1994) have presented research showing areas of consumer behavior in which older adults differ, and have discussed theories of human behavior that might offer insights into the reasons for consumer behavior in later life. The present research has used such information to develop a model that integrates theories and research findings into a life-stage model. "Life stages" are defined as states that characterize human development and aging, and derive from various aging processes and experiences.

The Life-Stage model was built on foundations of theories and research findings regarding behavior in later life. It is not simply based on any single assumption about behavior. Rather, the model takes into account all relevant explanations and data that offer insights into the behavior of older people in the marketplace. Much of the research in social sciences to be presented in this chapter shows that people age not just biologically or physically, but also psychologically, socially, and even spiritually; they age differently and at different rates. It will be argued, based on these findings, that it is often the composite of changes in these aging processes that affects consumer behavior, as in the case of retirement and becoming a grandparent; or it could be a chronic condition (e.g., arthritis) that can slow one down and make a person feel the need for certain products. Such events can occur at different stages in life, or they may never occur in some people, causing them to make the transisition into a given life stage and to experience subsequent needs for products and services.

The purpose of this chapter is to present relevant research from various fields of social science in order to establish the thesis that consumer behavior in later life is the outcome of various aging processes and circumstances people are likely to experience. Specifically, it discusses the theoretical foundations of the Life-Stage model by presenting scientific explanations of human behavior, and points to areas of consumer behavior in later life to which such explanations may apply.

CONCEPTIONS OF AGING

Behavior in later life is believed to be the outcome of aging processes and experiences over the life span that differ due to dynamic historical and cultural contexts in which individuals are embedded. It is widely accepted that people age as biological beings, social beings, and psychological beings (Moody 1988). *Biological aging* refers to the changes in human functional capacity due to changes in cells and tissues, causing deterioration of the biological system and its subsystems and susceptibility to disease and mortality. Thus, biological aging is due to natural changes (e.g., reduced rate of cell reproduction) and the result of disease (Cristofalo 1988). Biological aging is likely to alter consumer needs and ability to function in the marketplace. Previous research (e.g., MacNeil and Teague 1987; Schewe 1988) has shown how the aging of the various biological systems can affect consumer behavior. For example, with increasing age, consumers have difficulty reading fine print on labels and opening packages and containers (Moschis 1992). *Psychological aging* refers to continuous growth or change in cognition (ability to think and reason) and personality. Understanding changes in cognition (e.g., cognitive abilities) would help us better understand the elderly person's ability to process information and their susceptibility to persuasion (e.g., Phillips and Sternthal 1977).

Finally, *social aging* refers to changes in social relationships that define social status within a society, power relationships within social groups (e.g., family), and various roles people are expected to play at various stages in life. Such changes are likely to affect a wide range of consumer behaviors, including buying-role structures in later life and consumer behaviors defined as normative expectations (e.g., acceptance of senior discounts).

The three conceptions of aging are interdependent and, therefore, useful not only in directly addressing various aspects of consumer behavior in later life, but also in helping us understand the indirect impact of a given type of aging on consumer behavior via its effects on other forms of aging. Biological aging can affect both psychological as well as social aging. It may limit psychological growth, although there appears to be no universal age-related deterioration of cognition, or fragmentation of the emotional system or structure of personality (Perlmutter 1988). Disease, especially those associated with later life (e.g., arthritis, incontinence), can have adverse effects on the person's self-concept (Atchley 1987) and could cause early retirement (Smedley 1975) and social withdrawal (Herzog et al. 1988), contributing to the aging person's social aging. Psychological aging, in turn, can affect both biological and social aging. For example, depression can lead to poor eating habits, which affect the person's biological system and its ability to fight disease (Letsou and Price 1987). Depression can also lead to withdrawal and social isolation, that is, social disengagement. Finally, social aging has implications for biological and psychological aging. For example, social isolation can alter food consumption habits directly by affecting nutrition, which relates to disease, as well as indirectly by affecting the person's psychological state (MacNeil and Teague 1987). Also, it has been shown that social isolation is associated with a decrease in motivation to shop, cook, and eat by oneself. Similarly, isolation may increase fear of crime and theft, contributing to restriction of shopping trips and changes in eating habits (cf. Natow and Heslin 1980).

In sum, the three aging processes are relevant to the study of consumer behavior because they produce certain changes that are either directly related to consumer behavior such as ability to process information, or they relate to factors such as personality and self-concept that influence consumer behavior. The preceding discussion suggests that a model of aging and consumer behavior should take into account not only the various perspectives on aging, but also how the various types of aging relate to consumer behavior, directly or indirectly, as well as the various types of consumer behavior each type of aging and aging theory may help explain.

THEORIES OF AGING

In order to better understand the reasons why people behave the way they do in later life, one must often rely on theories of aging. These theories offer explanations for observed patterns of thought and action. Because there can be more than one explanation, there is often more than one theory that can be used to explain aging and age-related behaviors. Similarly, people age differently and we cannot assume that one person's behavior can be explained the same way as another person's behavior because they happen to be of the same age or have experienced similar circumstances. Thus, in order to study human behavior in later life, one must not only use appropriate theories, but must also recognize individual differences in aging, that is, biological, psychological, and social. One must assess the person's "position" in the aging continuum and use proper theoretical perspectives to explain one's behavior. This calls for measurement of various types of aging, as well as for deep understanding of aging theories.

Conceptions of, and explanations for, aging and age-related behaviors in later life are multidimensional in nature and have come from several disciplines. Appendix A summarizes definitions, measures, and perspectives on three types of aging: biological, psychological, and social aging.

Biological

Biological perspectives on life course focus on changes in human functional capacity due to changes in cells and tissues. Many of these changes are studied within the context of biological theories of aging, which consist of two kinds: (1) programming theories, which assume that aging is intrinsic, genetic, and developmental—a natural and expected result written into the genes; and (2) environmental theories (also known as error and stochastic), which assume that the rate of aging on a given organism depends on the accumulation of environmental insults that cause damage to the body's cells, resulting in malfunction of cells, molecules, and organs (e.g., Cristofalo 1988; Shock 1977; Whitbourne 1985).

Although the field of biology is rich in theories (Cristofalo 1988), we are far from finding answers to the aging process that would help us understand the person's physical growth, declining abilities, and the nature of disease and disorders commonly associated with aging (e.g., arthritis). However, the health condition of the biological system can be determined to some extent. There are several measurement models presently available (Dean 1988) that derive biological age from weighted equations (regression models) using performance measures of different bodily systems, although there is considerable debate over the specific systems (e.g., nervous, cardiovascular) that should be used and the specific measurement instruments that are most valid.

Recent efforts to understand biological processes over the life span incorporate variables from several disciplines. For example, Buhler (1968), one of the first students of the life course, distinguished five major biological phases of physical growth and reproductive ability, with these phases setting broad limits to mental abilities and social roles people occupy. Similarly, a framework that has been considered relatively fruitful in incorporating multidisciplinary perspectives involves empirical research that focuses on one substantive concern (life expectancy) as a function of biological, social, and psychological factors (Passuth and Bengtson 1988). Although the latter empirical approach does not account for the interactional features of the aging processes and reduces the aging process into one dependent variable, it represents a major step toward the development of multidisciplinary theories of aging (Yates 1988).

The aging of the various biological systems can affect consumer behavior in later life. Biological aging is likely to alter consumer needs and ability to function in the marketplace, creating opportunities for developing or modifying products, messages, and retail environments to better satisfy them. For example, changes in architectural design and store layout could be made to assist the older person to identify and remove merchandise from shelves (e.g., Pirki and Babic 1988). Several other aspects of consumption in later life can be examined from a biological or geriatric perspective. For example, preferences for certain products and services (e.g., disposable underwear for those who suffer from incontinence, dietary foods for those who suffer from diabetes) can be predicted rather accurately from health statistics on the aged population. The changing composition of the aging population can further help us determine the types of marketing and home environments (e.g., lighting, temperatures, packaging, labeling) most likely to be in demand. However, unlike previous research that suggests product-mix changes to compensate for physiological changes, more direct measures of physiological changes should be related to consumer behavior. For example, anthropometric changes (body shape and size) and changes in health conditions of various bodily systems should be used to tap biological changes. The implication for model building to explain consumer behavior in later life is that a wide variety of measures that tap the health conditions of the various bodily systems should be used.

Psychological

Psychological aging refers to continuous growth or change in cognition (mental activities) and personality. Views on how cognition and personality change with age vary, but most views focus on the person, the environment, or both (dialectic) (cf. Perlmutter 1988).

Cognitive Models. Views on cognition and cognitive development have traditionally been based on the processing-resource framework, which conceptualizes age-related declines in memory, intelligence, problem solving, and reasoning in terms of deficits in processing resources—that is, *resource deficit models*, ignoring the contextual and dialectic processes of development. According to processing-resource theorists, mental activities require varying amounts of cognitive resources, which are limited and show a wide individual variation. Such resource variations depend on specific points in time, maximum allotment, and they show decline in later life (Light 1988). Recent mounting evidence primarily from longitudinal studies, however, suggests that it is possible to continue improvement of existing cognitive skills and acquisition of compensatory and new cognitive skills throughout life (Perlmutter 1988; Willis and Schaie 1988). This improvement may reflect higher education, increased societal roles, or increase in the level of intellectual stimulation in one's environment (e.g., learning to use home computers). A field study of acceptance of new technologies found that factors such as previous familiarity with other technologies, education, interest in technological products, and lifestyles might be good predictors of the older person's adoption of such innovations, regardless of age (Moschis and Sachdev 1991).

Cognitive models can be used by consumer researchers to study a wide variety of consumer-related cognitions such as those related to consumer-information processing and problem solving. Variables related to consumer perceptions, evaluation of commercial stimuli, information recall and use (e.g., John and Cole 1986) are examples of factors that could be studied using cognitive models. However, unlike previous studies that have confined explanation to rather narrowly defined measures of cognitive aging (derived from deficit models) (e.g.,

Cole and Gaeth 1990), a wider variety of measures of cognitive aging have been suggested (Salthouse 1991; Schaie 1987). The implication for model building is that in order to explain mental activities in later life, one must include measures that tap the older person's previous experiences and expertise.

Development of Personality and Self. While models of cognition appear to be directly relevant to the study of consumer mental processes, models of personality and self help us understand the development of factors which might affect consumer behavior. Thus, the task at hand is not only to identify or understand changes in personality and self, but also to relate them to consumer behavior.

Social scientists have examined the development of personality and self throughout life by focusing on either stages or processes of development. The idea that people go through *stages of development* constitutes a central core of stage theories. For example, Erikson's theory focuses on how people develop an identity in childhood and adolescence as well as in middle and late life. According to Erikson, qualities formed in early life are likely to affect the person's behavior in later life. Unless a person learns to establish intimacy (close personal relationships) in early adulthood, he or she cannot establish generativity in middle adulthood (caring for the young and the world one lives in), which is prerequisite to the development of integrity in late life (Erikson 1963).

Empirical research has generally employed these concepts in ex post facto fashion—that is, they are used to interpret obtained findings rather than to rely on the formation of research designs or measurement instruments (Atchley 1987; Ryff 1982). Data in the consumer field can be interpreted in line with this framework. For example, when older adults were asked in a recent study by Marriott Corporation about their unfulfilled aspirations, two-thirds wished they had helped society more during their lives (Dodd 1990). Such a wish is in line with the development of generativity, and may explain their inclination to give large portions of their income to charities (Moschis 1992), since generativity would lead to integrity—that is, help them feel more at ease with themselves in late life.

Explanations of consumer behavior in later life based on stage theories appear to be intuitively appealing. However, one must keep in mind that these theories have not been empirically tested, and have been severely criticized. These stage theories, where the highest stage might be thought to consist of "ego-integrity," "self-actualization," or "ego-transcendence," have been criticized within the cognitive and life-span developmental domains. Not only do they represent an inflexible formulation, requiring developmental progressions that are unidirectional, irreversible, hierarchical, invariant, and universal, but such rigid models also ignore a multiplicity of influences surrounding development such as cohort effects and individual differences (e.g., Dowd 1987; Moody 1988; Ryff 1982). These criticisms weaken the value of stage models as tools for prediction and control. However, stage models maintain their value as heuristic tools because they can be used as frameworks for interpreting consumer data. Thus, consumer researchers could benefit from stage theories when using the humanistic approach to study consumer behavior.

Process theories of human development, on the other hand, view development as a continuous, gradual, and smooth transition from one state to the next. The *cognitive personality theory* advanced by Thomae (1970) views personality in a multitheoretical context, emphasizing the interaction of environment and self (perceptions of reality) in an ongoing dialectical context defined by individual and social constraints. Emphasis is placed on the older person's coping strategies, the objective features of the environment, and social competence or incompetence, all of which require assessment in a situation. Thus, personality is the outcome of these processes and strategies.

Because the theory is concerned with the individual's way of perceiving reality and responding in a manner consistent with his or her own perceptions, this theory comes closest to providing explanations of consumer behavior in later life than other personality theories of aging. For example, the motive toward achieving consistency within one's overall conceptualization of self can be traced to the works of self theorists and psychoanalysts; it implies a tendency to act in line with one's self-concept. Rosenberg (1979) suggests that the power and persistence of the self-consistency motive is strong enough to keep people from changing their self-views developed in early life, when such views would not be considered valid by others, such as thinking young and not ''acting one's age.'' This motive might also explain the older person's propensity to use products and services aimed at helping the aging person maintain his/her youthful image (such as anti-aging skin creams, health spas, and cosmetic surgery) (Dychtwald and Flower 1989); and it might explain the failure of products such as ''Affinity'' shampoo (created to deal with the problems of over-40 hair) and Kellogg's cereal ''40+.''

Dychtwald and Flower (1989) cite examples of implications for marketers of this type of research. For example, one could market to segments defined by cognitive age rather than chronological age and develop advertising appeals without having to deal with consumers' psychological acceptance or rejection of their chronological age. Furthermore, consumer researchers could identify products that are associated with older age as well as products and brand names that are age-irrelevant and promote a positive self-image. Such research could help marketers better position their products and services to appeal to the aging population.

The self-consistency motive is just one of the many domains that can be used to predict the aging person's consumer behavior. Other tenets of the cognitive personality theory could be used. For example, perceived decline in social competence due to physiological changes may create the need to remain independent. The motive to remain independent as well as other psychological motives (e.g., security) could be used to explain consumer behavior. Schewe (1991) shows how such information could benefit marketers and advertisers, and gives several examples of product positioning and advertising appeals that could be developed for the older consumer market.

Continuity theory suggests that the personality formed early in life continues throughout the life span without major changes. According to the theory, middle-aged and older adults attempt to deal with changes associated with aging by using strategies tied to their past experiences of themselves and their social world (Atchley 1989). While the theory suggests a static view of aging, recent conceptions of continuity theory differentiate between a basic structure which persists over time and a dynamic view which recognizes a variety of changes within the context provided by the basic structure (Atchley 1989). Using the psychometric approach, Neugarten (1977) found that among the many dimensions of personality studied, only introversion changes with age, in that there is an inward orientation which reflects self-acceptance and understanding (or, in Erikson's terms, "integrity") rather than social withdrawal or disengagement; and those components of personality that have been important to the individual's identity tend to intensify throughout later life. Such changes have implications for consumer behavior. For example, one could speculate that growing integrity and self-acceptance might be manifested into less conspicuous and more functional or utilitarian consumption.

Another model more familiar to consumer researchers is VALS (Values and Lifestyles) and its recent revision (VALS2), as well as its version applicable to older adults—LAVOA (Lifestyles and Values of Older Americans). The model is originally based on Maslow's stage theory of human needs, and uses personality characteristics to form segments of consumers.

While previous research on personality has not been very successful in predicting consumer behavior (Kassarjian and Sheffet 1991), more recent research suggests that personality may be related only to those consumer behaviors which are directly relevant to satisfying consumer needs. For example, one useful hypothesis is that the older person's media use is functionally related to one's information needs (O'Guinn and Faber 1991). Swank (1979) found that the elderly's need levels were systematically related to certain activities for fulfillment of needs. These findings suggest that personality and subsequent behaviors may change only in response to biophysical, psychological, and social aging, with personality changes reflecting adjustment to old age. Thus, one can speculate that personality characteristics ("traits") sensitive to aging (e.g., introversion) may be better predictors of consumer behavior than traits less sensitive to aging (e.g., traditionalism). The implication for model building to explain consumer behavior in later life is that one should use personality characteristics that are sensitive to aging.

Sociological

Passuth and Bengtson (1988) note that "sociological theories of aging have emerged, implicitly or explicitly, from five general sociological perspectives:

structural functionalism, symbolic interactionism, exchange, Marxism, and social phenomenology'' (p. 334). Coming from diverse theoretical perspectives, the specific theories differ and are useful in explaining different aspects of human behavior. This section presents sociological perspectives on aging according to the general sociological perspective from which they have derived (see Appendix A). Although some of the early theories (e.g., activity, disengagement) have also emerged from these sociological perspectives, these theories are not discussed in great detail since they have largely been discredited because they are not susceptible to falsification (Moody 1988) and do not meet the criteria of a theory (Burbank 1986; Hendricks and Hendricks 1977; Passuth and Bengtson 1988).

Structural Functionalism. Structural functionalism argues that social behavior is best understood from the perspective of the equilibrium needs of the social system. Social behavior is viewed in terms of its function within the structure of society. Key concepts include norms, roles, and socialization. Norms are socially accepted rules about behavior, roles are behavioral expectations that constitute a particular status, and socialization is the process by which individuals learn to internalize the norms and values of society. Structural functionalism is the underlying theme of several social theories of aging, including age-stratification, modernization, and disengagement.

Age-stratification theory acknowledges age as a hierarchy of age strata, each consisting of obligations and prerogatives assigned to members as they move from one stratum to the next. Each age stratum is expected to develop its own characteristic subculture as it moves through time (Riley, Johnson, and Foner 1972). Age norms are conveyed to them through socialization, although people often anticipate and learn age-related changes before they encounter them (Atchley 1987). The model specifies antecedents and processes leading to the older person's change in social lifestyles and the assumption of social roles ''appropriate'' for older people. For example, research studies show that appropriate roles for grandparents include dispensing services and material supports and engaging in certain expressive activities, but never interfering with the authority of their adult offspring (Wood 1971).

In the field of consumer behavior, Mathur (1991) used specific components of the model (socialization processes expressed as instrumental and basic care) to study anticipatory consumer socialization for old age among younger adults providing care to older relatives. Also, data presented by Wagner and Hanna (1983) suggest that persons approaching retirement are likely to reduce their clothing expenditures in anticipation of change in roles (that is, anticipatory socialization).

Finally, a study by Jache (1986) provides evidence of reverse socialization (that is, parent socializes the child for old age). Age stratification theory can be a useful framework for studying select aspects of consumer behavior that can be defined in the context of broader social roles where societal expectations exist. For example, Moschis, Mathur, and Smith (1993) used this theory to explain older consumers' responses to age-based marketing offerings, assuming the acceptance of some of these offerings is beneficial from the older consumer's point of view and, therefore, socially desirable.

The transition into many other social roles appropriate for people in later stages of life could be studied within this framework. For example, roles in later life might include the roles of the empty-nester, caregiver, retiree, grandparent, and widower (Schewe and Balazs 1992). The assumption of some of these roles involves a smooth and gradual process and are considered to be normal life-stage changes. For example, research suggests that people begin preparing for retirement in their early forties (Riley et al. 1969). The assumption of other roles such as "widowhood" may be more abrupt and "off-stage" (Murrell, Norris, and Grote 1988).

As people assume new roles, they tend to redefine their consumption needs and priorities. For example, many marketers have focused on providing products and services (e.g., travel) to take up the retiree's newfound time. Similarly, many toy marketers target grandparents (Schewe and Balazs 1992). Thus, marketers can benefit from studying the aging person's transition into various roles to better segment and target their markets, position their products, and facilitate role adaptation. Role adaptation could be facilitated by various mechanisms. AT&T, for example, has recently begun a program that provides information to its employees who are caregivers for older relatives to help them effectively perform this role. The implication for model building is that researchers must use variables that are major markers for transitions into major roles, since older consumer behavior can vary by type of role one has experienced.

Modernization theory is based on structural functionalism aimed at explaining social behavior from the standpoint of the needs of the social system (Cowgill 1974). The theory suggests that the status of older people derives from their relationship to evolving systems of social roles, which vary across societies, depending on the degree of industrialization or modernization. The status of the older person, the theory argues, is inversely related to the level of industrialization of a particular social system (e.g., culture, country). Theoretically, the age of the population is an important variable. Industrialized countries have lower fertility and mortality rates and larger segments of elderly population than less industrialized countries.

Studies on modernization theory have focused primarily on economic status (income and buying power) (e.g., Harris 1986) rather than on consumption (e.g., expenditure patterns). Modernization theory can address consumer-related issues at the macro-level. For example, one can speculate that in less developed or developing societies, where the elderly enjoy a higher status, images or stereotypes of older models in ads would be more positive than in industrialized societies. Similarly, one would expect to find a larger number of welfare programs among the more industrialized than among the less industrialized countries. These and other similar macro-issues could be addressed in the context of modernization theory. Because our focus is on market segmentation of the older consumer market in this country, modernization theory does not appear to be relevant to market segmentation

Disengagement theory argues that the elderly and society engage in mutual withdrawal until a new equilibrium is reached that is mutually satisfying. Although the theory has been under severe criticism and has largely been discredited, elements of this perspective have been revived and have focused on understanding the elderly's exclusion from valued social roles (Passuth and Bengtson 1988). Although society has few explicit consumption roles where exclusion of the elderly is desirable, business and societal efforts to provide incentives that encourage changes in the elderly's consumer behaviors (e.g., senior shopping days, reduced bus fare) suggest that such changes may be mutually satisfying to the elderly and society.

Symbolic Interactionism. Contrary to structural functionalism, which argues that an individual becomes his or her role, the symbolic interactionist perspective views aging persons as active participants in a "role-taking" process, adjusting their behavior according to the responses of others. The *social breakdown* (SB) model addresses the issue of how the environment may bring about changes in the older person's self-concept. This model is based upon the premise that an older person approaching old age experiences lack of defined guidelines, role loss, normlessness, and lack of reference groups; and in the absence of direction, the older person becomes susceptible to negative labels assigned by others. Older persons gradually, almost inadvertently, adopt some of the negative characteristics ascribed to them, thus slipping deeper into a dependent status as the cycle is repeated. The spiraling breakdown of competence in elderly individuals can be reversed by improving environmental support and facilitating an expression of personal strength (Kuypers and Bengtson 1973).

The SB model borrows from several other theories in attempting to explain the interdependence between older adults and their social environments, especially *labeling theory* in sociology and psychiatry (Passuth and Bengtson 1988). It offers sociological explanations for changes in the older person's psychological state (self-concept, competence), although the model recognizes the dynamic interplay between sociological theories (social learning and role theory) and psychological theories (e.g., self-consistency). This perspective differs from earlier theoretical traditions (e.g., Cooley's "looking-glass" self) and more recent psychological perspectives (e.g., cognitive personality theory) in that a greater emphasis is placed on the person's social environment in bringing about changes, the processes by which change occurs—that is, social and self (private) labeling, and the required conditions or moderators for changes in self-concept.

While the SB model appears to hold promise in helping us understand why the older person's self-concept changes in later life, and the consumption-related consequences of such changes, its usefulness remains questionable. Although cross-sectional data on the elderly's labeling and perceptions of the elderly on TV relate to their self-concept (Korzenny and Neuendorf 1980; Rodin and Langer 1980), the antecedents, processes, and outcomes are likely to be inseparable in cross-sectional data, raising reliability and validity issues. At best, the model presently serves as a framework for interpreting consumer data rather than a vehicle for empirical research.

Subculture theory asserts the development of a distinctive aged subculture. Rose (1965) advocated this theory, contending that whenever members of one category interact more among themselves than with people from other categories, a subculture will be formed. Certain factors are likely to facilitate the interaction among the aged, such as living in close proximity (e.g., retirement communities), while other factors inhibit the aged person's ability to maintain interaction with younger members of society (e.g., mandatory retirement). In addition, social services designed for older people by organizations such as AARP make them aware of their common situation, contributing to their group or status consciousness (Karp 1988). The theory's implication for consumer behavior model building is that the mature market is a homogeneous one, but different from the younger consumer market. The aged population's consumer behaviors may differ from those of younger consumers, but the theory leaves much to be desired with respect to our ability to understand the processes that lead to the formation of this subculture and the heterogeneity of the older population as consumers.

Activity theory states that, in order to maintain a positive self, elderly persons must substitute new roles for those lost in old age (e.g., roles of worker and spouse). This effort to stay ''engaged'' has been offered as an explanation of the older person's need to maintain high levels of social activity and the assumption of new ones (e.g., volunteering). For example, Mathur and his colleagues (1992) found that the main motivation for giving one's money, time, and possessions to charities was social. Activity theory appears to be relevant to the study of the older person's development of new consumption patterns such as volunteering, adult education, and religiosity found among the aged (Atchley 1987).

In sum, symbolic interactionism theories have little value in empirical research; variables for these theories cannot be easily used as explanatory factors in a model of older consumer behavior.

Exchange Theory. This theory attempts to explain the elderly's shrinking networks as a realignment of their personal relationships. According to the exchange theory, social life is a series of social exchanges that add and subtract from one's depository of power and prestige. Power derives from imbalance of social exchange, with the participant who values rewards more highly losing power, and the other participant gaining it (Dowd 1975).

Exchange theory has been applied to the field of aging to explain visiting patterns of family members (Martin 1971), and to analyze the relationships in traditional and caregiving homesharing arrangements (Danigelis and Fengler 1990), and more recently to the field of consumer behavior to explain the older person's propensity to save (Wallace and Mathur 1990) and give gifts to charities and relatives (e.g., Mathur, Smith, and Moschis 1992). The theory might be particularly useful in explaining realignment in role relationships due to changes in power and resources associated with retirement (e.g., reduced income), such as sex roles associated with family decisions. For example, studies show that upon retirement, men and women become egalitarian in decision making (Heslop and Marshall 1991; Moschis 1987). This may be due to the husband's loss of power and reduced resources (fixed income) that he had maintained as a productive worker and breadwinner during his life, and to the quality of the resource-based power between spouses (Atchley 1987; Heslop and Marshall 1991). Thus, one can speculate that the older person's participation in family consumer decisions and the influence other family members have upon his/her consumer decisions are inversely related to his/her ability to provide economic resources and social support to family members.

The theory might also be useful in explaining realignment in consumption-related sex-role relationships due to physiological changes in men and women. Men's life expectancy is six years shorter than that of women, and men tend to marry chronologically younger women. Thus, the older man is more likely to become physically dependent upon his spouse, and older women are more likely to experience widowhood than their male counterparts.

The marketing implications of research into changes in sex-role relationships in later life are rather obvious. Marketers would have to redefine the target market of older consumers responsible for decisions traditionally made by the husband (e.g., home repairs, financial decisions). Since older women must learn to play new roles, they need to be socialized to effectively assume more demanding consumer roles than they used to play. This could have implications for the need to educate older female consumers about nontraditional purchasing decisions. For example, financial-service providers could provide investment seminars to older women in their communities. Exchange theory's implication for model building is that variables that serve as markers of transition into new roles, such as retirement and widowhood, should be considered, since the assumption of new roles correlates with changes in consumer behaviors.

Marxism. Marx's theories of capitalistic development argue that the social distribution of power and resources in a capitalistic society is embedded within the context of social relations of production (cf. Passuth and Bengtson 1988). Drawing upon Marxism, the *political economy perspective* focuses on the state in relation to the economy in a capitalistic society to explain the plight of the elderly. It suggests that programs designed for the elderly (e.g., home-delivered meals, case management services) are much more beneficial to capitalist interests than to the elderly themselves, helping to increase the number of service-oriented jobs.

The political economy perspective can be applied to address public policy issues confronting the elderly, especially with respect to federal programs. Distributing federal monies to the elderly via ''nonprofit'' service agencies, as opposed to providing these resources to the elderly's family caregivers, may be viewed in the context of this perspective. Thus, we can speculate that the more capitalistic a society, the greater the proportion of resources distributed to the elderly via social service agencies. As it deals with macro-level issues, this theory has few implications for market-segmentation model building.

Social Phenomenology. Social phenomenology is broadly used to include a variety of works, especially the *phenomenology* of Schutz (1967) and the *ethnomethodology* of Garfinkel (1967). This perspective examines the process by which meanings are socially constructed, focusing on language and knowledge as constitutive elements of everyday life (Passuth and Bengtson 1988). Rather than being concerned with the definitional nature of social life, social phenomenology examines the emergent, situational, and constitutive elements of aging experience, with "the meaning of aging presented and negotiated from moment to moment as people participate in sometimes elusive, but serious conversation" (Gubrium and Buckholdt 1977, p. viii). Thus, for example, the meaning of an individual's behavior for others depends on how they conceptualize it, and may vary according to the observer's perceptions of the individual's age. Thus, it appears that social phenomenology has little value in the construction of market-segmentation models.

MULTITHEORETICAL MODELS

Despite merits of traditional theoretical approaches discussed in the previous section, none of them can completely explain consumer behavior in later life. As the discussion suggests, some aspects of consumer behavior can be explained by (or understood in the context of) certain theories, while other dimensions of consumer behavior can be better studied using other theoretical perspectives. Concerns with the fragmentation of knowledge and lack of cross-fertilization among various disciplines have led several researchers of human behavior to develop models that integrate the various theoretical perspectives. One recent multitheoretical model consistent with this development is the use of a life-course perspective, an approach that is reflected in recent theoretical formulations of biologists (e.g., Cristofalo 1988), anthropologists (e.g., Fry 1988), psychologists (e.g., Perlmutter 1988), sociologists (e.g., Hagestad and Neugarten 1985; Riley, Johnson, and Foner 1972), as well as those who subscribe to humanistic approaches, whether these are dialectic (e.g., Riegel 1976), interpretive (e.g., Reker and Wong 1988), or critical in nature (Moody 1988). The life-course perspective is also seen by economists as potentially useful in "the understanding of the labor market, the allocation of time and goods, and the role of the future life time as individuals make economic and consumption decisions" (Baltes, Reese, and Lipsitt 1980, p. 100).

The Concept of Life Course

The study of life course cuts across several disciplines. It refers to the study of human development viewed biologically, psychologically, and socially (Clau-

sen 1986). The definition of the life course varies with the disciplinary background of the investigator. Psychologists usually refer to life-span development,
focusing a great deal of attention on intrapsychic phenomena (George 1982).
Sociologists, on the other hand, concentrate on age-related transitions that are
socially created, socially recognized, and socially shared (Hagestad and Neugarten 1985). Others use the term interchangeably to refer to both human development and social processes extending over the individual's life span or over
significant portions of it (e.g., Mayer and Tuma 1990).

Clausen (1986) views life course as ''a progression through time,'' recognizing three components of time: life time, social time, and historical time. *Life
time* or aging refers to the biological or physiological changes of the body or
its systems and the onset of disease. *Social time* is defined as ''a set of norms
that specify when particular life transitions or accomplishments are expected to
occur in a particular society or social milieu'' (p. 2). Finally, *historical time*
mirrors societal change, epoch-making events, and cultural eras. The focus is
on movement and transitions of individuals and groups (cohorts) that experience
a given event or set of circumstances. Clausen's conception of the life course
does not deal exclusively with the psychological component of life-span development. Instead, the psychological dimension is viewed to be a part of the
biological component.

Parallel to the three components of time, three general perspectives on life
course have been advanced (Clausen 1986). The *developmental perspective*
seeks to explain physiological and psychological changes that occur with the
accumulation or diminution of time. Physiological changes describe the aging
process that results in the physical development and deterioration of the biological system, while psychological changes assume a degree of ''unfolding'' of
potential that exists in the organism (Clausen 1986). The *socialization perspective* stresses the importance of the demands that other members of society make
upon the individual. Through the process of socialization, such demands shape
attitudes, interests, and values, and provide motivations for learning new skills
over the person's life course. Finally, the *adaptation perspective* views the life
course as a sequence of adaptations to events and circumstances. These adaptations are needed not only because of specific events and circumstances an
individual may experience over one's life course, but also because of developmental and social changes. As Clausen puts it:

One must adapt not only to the socially patterned demands of others, but also to one's
growth and developmental problems, to changing life conditions and relationships, to
frustration and losses, to illness, and, if we survive long enough, to declining strength
and abilities. (p. 17)

Thus, in the context of these diverse perspectives, behavior over the life
course could be studied as an outgrowth of developmental changes, as an out-

come of socialization, and as a consequence of adaptations to specific events and circumstances that have taken place or are anticipated.

Life-course research began developing as an interdisciplinary program of study during the 1980s (Mayer and Tuma 1990). While this framework has been used in various disciplines to study a variety of social behaviors such as job entry, retirement, relocation, and marital formation, the approach lends itself to the examination of several other aspects of an individual's behavior (Mayer and Tuma 1990).

Life-course research has several precursors, including studies of social mobility, aging, and social biography. While studies of social mobility compare members of two or more generations (or members of the same generations at a few points in time), the life course advocates that social mobility should be conceived as event histories, that is, sequences of moves and events unfolding over time (Mayer and Tuma 1990). Similarly, in comparison to most theories of aging that stress the self-contained nature of age differentiation and age norms, the life course emphasizes the historical perspective of aging, raising issues of multiple time dimensions, not age per se. Finally, contemporary methodology (event history analysis) makes the distinction between biographical studies (many variables on few cases) and social demography (few variables on many cases) obsolete, since life-course analysis can combine the advantages of a large representative sample and compatibility of measurement with many of the advantages provided by the multivariate richness of individual biographies (Mayer and Tuma 1990).

Life-Course Perspectives

Because life course entails development, socialization, and adaptation, any adequate explanation of the individual's behavior must incorporate elements of all of these perspectives. Attempts to combine these elements have been influenced by theory and research in various disciplines. This section reviews main frameworks of life course developed in different disciplines, interprets consumer research in the context of these models, and discusses select areas of marketing and consumer behavior to which these frameworks may apply.

Developmental. Developmental perspectives on life course are based on theories of cognition and personality. To facilitate inquiry into psychological growth and integrate the various cognitive psychological perspectives, Perlmutter (1988) proposed a multidisciplinary framework that takes into account biological factors, environmental factors (both physical and social), and cognitive factors, in a *three-tier model of cognition.* The first tier incorporates basic mechanisms, primary mental functions, and fluid abilities. This tier is susceptible to deterioration associated with programmed biological aging and health problems. The second tier of the cognitive system incorporates what has been known as world knowledge and crystallized abilities. This tier derives from environmental experience and is assumed to be a psychological addition to the biological layer.

It is immune to deterioration associated with programmed biological aging, but is capable of adapting to the environment.

The third tier incorporates what has been referred to as strategies and higher mental functions. This tier is also immune to biological fluctuations and emerges out of the organism's cognition about its own activity. For example, Salthouse (1985) reports one of his studies where although basic reaction time of older typists was slower than that of younger typists, older typists were able to maintain comparable typing skills by reading farther ahead. Thus, cognitive development is recognized as a separate process resulting from internal experiences of the cognitive system, a layer of the cognitive system emerging from the system's own activity. The idea that cognition becomes the object of itself reflects contemporary thinking among developmental psychologists and sociologists (e.g., Dowd 1987; Flavell 1977). This process is similar to Piaget's (1983) "reflective abstraction" and what Flavell (1977) refers to as "metacognition." Thus, according to this model, performance of some basic cognitive processes may be affected by the deterioration of the biological system that supports cognition, but the cognitive system also seems to be capable of adapting itself to environmental circumstances it encounters. Experience incorporated in thought and decision may compensate for processing limitations due to biological declines—a notion consistent with data presented by Phillips and Sternthal (1977). Even some cognitive processes are expected to improve with age. This last view focuses attention on factors that *mediate* change in functioning, specifically on variables such as health, personality, attitudes, social roles, and lifestyles.

Perlmutter (1988) provides evidence supporting the three-tier model. In the field of consumer behavior, much research provides evidence (inferred from cross-sectional studies) in support of Tier I, suggesting a decline in mental functioning due to biological aging (Phillips and Sternthal 1977). The results of two studies provide evidence in support of Tier II. Specifically, a study by Gaeth and Heath (1987) found that training in late life can decrease susceptibility to misleading advertising among older adults, while a study by Cole and Gaeth (1990) showed that older people can improve their ability to use complex decision rules. Perlmutter's model poses challenges to consumer researchers to seek more advanced forms of consumer skills and thought processes (Tier III). For example, older adults may utilize more efficient information processing strategies by relating present information to established cognitive schemata or by "chunking" (grouping) information more effectively.

In order to integrate the various theoretical *perspectives on personality*, Lerner (1988) presents a model of the development of personality structure across life. He argues that individuals possess structural and functional characteristics are universal (nomothetic-generic); common to some but not to all others (nomothetic-differential); and unique (ipsative-idiographic). Universal characteristics are posited by stage approaches to the development of personality structure and function (e.g., Erikson 1959) which are genetic and invariant stage progressions, and provide adaptive means for people to meet cultural and societal demands.

Nomothetic-differential characteristics have been the domain of the differential approach to personality development; although the array of contexts and events experienced by each person is unique, some clusterings across individuals exist due to common experiences (e.g., culture, historical epoch, religion). This approach is exemplified in the work of Baltes and Featherman (e.g., Baltes, Reese, and Lipsitt 1980; Featherman and Lerner 1985). Furthermore, the social embeddedness that produces both unique and common attributes of personality relates to continuity and discontinuity in personality development. Because of the relative plasticity of humans, each person becomes unique because of the unique time-ordered set of contexts, events, roles, and groups to which one is exposed over the life course.

Finally, the ipsative approach has a strong empirical basis in human biology: one's biological genotype exists in reciprocal relation with one's social genotype, producing a unique individual. "Different genes come into play at various times during life, making the expression of any individual human genotype a developmental phenomenon" (Lerner 1988, p. 30). Human genetic individuality is enhanced by its development character. Not only are there an estimated 70 trillion potential human prototypes, making "the likelihood of anyone ever—in the past, present, or future—having the same genotype as anyone else . . . dismissably small" (McClearn 1981, p. 19), but also the organism's context may produce a different functional genotype at different times in the life span.

In sum, Lerner (1988) argues that individuals possess structural characteristics that are unique, common to some but not all others, and are universal. Individuality in personality is the result of humans' plasticity across life, which is enabled ontogenetically by one's genetic, neuroanatomical, and neurochemical attributes; these attributes constitute the basis of human responsivity to environment (sets of groups, events, and roles to which one is exposed). It is this responsivity which affects development over the life course along dimensions of both constancy-change and commonality-singularity. Based on these arguments, Lerner develops a model and presents supportive data to promote longitudinal, change-sensitive, multi-level, and multivariate research orientation in ecologically meaningful settings.

Lerner's (1988) model serves as a useful framework for integrating various approaches to studying personality development, and the model's demonstrated value is "its ability to integrate a broad range of phenomena pertinent to a multi-level, multi-process view of personality" (p. 42). It is particularly relevant to the study of the individual's personality over the life course because it provides a "framework that is richly generative of a new set of empirical findings linking individuals to their contexts across their lives" (p. 42).

Although previous research on personality has not examined the relationship between personality and consumer behavior over the life span, more recent efforts to causally link personality to behavior over the life course (the choices individuals make at various age-related transition points, and the level of adaptation in new settings) suggest potentially useful avenues for studying the effects of personality on consumer behavior over the life course (Caspi and Elder 1988).

Socialization. Sociologists have used the life-course approach to study age-related transitions across socially recognized turning points that provide road maps for human lives and outline life paths. The social structuring of life time is a compelling human need to define the predictability of life; it helps a person plot where one is and where he or she yet may go by examining culturally constructed age-based schedules (Hagestad and Neugarten 1985).

Although the life-course approach has been linked to the sociology of age, it has its roots in anthropology and social psychology. Anthropologists were the first to examine how societies create age-related transitions and assign social meaning to the passage of time, while social-psychologists have examined common ways members of a society think of age-related transitions over the life course (Hagestad and Neugarten 1985).

Sociological theories of the life course view the individual in terms of social roles one occupies. Although entry into a major role may indicate attainment of a developmental stage, the acquisition of such roles does not necessarily occur in an invariant order. Stages defined by roles are descriptive categories with theoretical explanations found in the processes of socialization, selection, and adaptation. Socialization has been the research focus of several writers in various areas of social sciences, including sociology, psychology, and anthropology (Moschis 1987). Most of the contributions to the field come from sociological perspectives, especially structural functionalism and symbolic interactionism.

The traditional view of the socialization perspective is that of normativity, since the dominant emphasis in socialization research has been the study of the processes that shape individuals into responsible members of society. Although this perspective has enjoyed a long-standing tradition in social sciences (e.g., Goslin 1969; Riley et al. 1969), it has received extensive criticisms from those using other perspectives, and several revisions have been proposed (Dannefer 1988). This perspective, as developed by communication and consumer behavior researchers (e.g., McLeod and O'Keefe 1972; Moschis 1987), suggests that behavior in late life develops or changes as a result of the older person's interaction with socialization agents (e.g., mass media), with social structural factors (e.g., social class), and developmental factors (e.g., age or life cycle), affecting behavior directly or indirectly via socialization agents. In this revised version, the socialization perspective has been used to study behaviors which are not part of socially prescribed roles such as political socialization (public affairs knowledge), mass media use (e.g., O'Guinn and Faber 1991), economic behavior (Denhardt and Jeffress 1971), as well as a wide range of consumer behaviors (e.g., Smith and Moschis 1990). Thus, a wide range of consumer behaviors could be studied using the socialization perspective.

While the traditional view of socialization stresses normativity (macro-level processes) and offers a vehicle for integrating normative developmental conceptions (e.g., disengagement), more recent formulations of the socialization perspective acknowledge the dynamics of micro-level processes addressed by symbolic interactionists (Dannefer 1988). The symbolic interaction version is acknowledged by treating socialization processes as reciprocal when the supposed socializer is recognized as not just a passive recipient but as a co-socializer (e.g., Dannefer 1988; Riley, Johnson, and Foner 1972). This expanded view of socialization provides a broader vehicle for integrating different perspectives on social aging such as exchange and symbolic interactionism (Mutran and Reitzes 1984). It helps modify theories relevant to stages in later life (e.g., subculture), which infer socialization from observed intragroup similarities by focusing on processes by which group consciousness develops (e.g., Sherman, Ward, and LaGory 1985). The socialization perspective, as developed by consumer behavior and communication researchers (e.g., McLeod and O'Keefe 1972; Moschis 1987), attempts to overcome the problem related to the assumption of age-stratification theory that "all cohorts experience aging the same way" by specifying the context (social structures, age, or life-cycle position) in which socialization takes place; and it focuses on the learning process (modeling, reinforcement, and social interaction) through which socialization takes place, offering greater specificity than many other sociological perspectives on aging (e.g., subculture, age stratification, activity) which infer socialization from less specified processes or from outcomes (behaviors). Consumer researchers have recently used this framework to integrate gerontological theories of aging (Smith and Moschis 1990) and to study older consumers' responses to age-targeted marketing stimuli (e.g., senior discounts) (Moschis, Mathur, and Smith 1993).

Adaptation. The adaptation perspective views the life course as a sequence of adaptations to events and circumstances. One must adapt to socially shared demands of others as well as to various unscheduled events and circumstances deriving from changing life conditions, psychological and biophysical changes that accompany aging and growth (Clausen 1986). Adaptation is particularly needed to cope with events or circumstances over which one has little control. Such events may be due to psychological, social, or environmental factors. For example, inability to reach major life goals and disruption of relations with others create stress. Coping with such stress and adapting more or less successfully to it is considered to be an important element in the life course (Clausen 1986). Vaillant (1977) elaborates on the importance of adaptation in the life course; he discusses how each person builds a unique set of strategies over the life course to cope with unacceptable and painful feelings, with such adaptive strategies likely to be shifted to reflect maturational development over the life course.

Hagestad and Neugarten (1985) differentiate between life-course analysis and life-event analysis. While life course focuses on turning points that are socially constructed and socially recognized (i.e., culturally constructed life schedules), many events may not be socially meaningful. Certain events serve as markers of transition between life stages, such as retirement, while others are not related to life stage, such as loss of a job; and others are normal but "off-stage," occurring either earlier than expected (e.g., death of a spouse at age 30), or later than expected (e.g., birth of a child at age 45) (Murrell, Norris, and Grote 1988). The *timing-of-events model* is based on the concept of social time, which defines the expected time for making major life transitions (Clausen 1986). Research has suggested that individual development over the life span is regulated not only by a biological clock (the ticking of which triggers changes in developmental processes), but also by a social chronograph that makes one aware of whether his or her major life goals are being accomplished within a socially normative span of time (e.g., Balkwell 1985).

Research studies have shown that young adults take on a number of life roles within a relatively short period of time (e.g., marriage, parenthood, job), while middle-aged and older adults experience role changes and losses (e.g., empty nest, retirement, death of parents and spouse) (Hughes, Blazer, and George 1988). Henderson, Byrne, and Duncan-Jones (1981) reported that younger persons, in comparison to their older counterparts, experience more events related to work, school, financial matters, legal matters, and changes in personal relationships and living conditions. Murrell and his associates (1988) present an argument put forth by Eysenck (1983) that prior exposure to stress assists in adaptation to later stress. Because of their longer life, older adults have had the opportunity to be exposed to changes, and they may draw upon prior experiences to better adapt to changes in later life.

Role transitions and adaptation to new life conditions have important implications for understanding age-related behaviors in later life for three reasons. First, people (through anticipatory socialization or rehearsal) prepare themselves for scheduled events and such anticipations drive present behaviors (e.g., retirement planning). Second, variability in role transitions may affect behavior and future role transitions. For example, early and prolonged entry into a nursing home (e.g., due to Alzheimer's disease) may deplete a family's lifetime savings and change post-retirement lifestyles. Finally, there are intra- and inter-cohort variations in transition patterns and their long-term consequences. For example, Elder's (1974) seminal work showed that the Great Depression did not affect all subgroups of a given cohort equally; there were long-term effects only on families with one-third drop in income, and these consequences were different across families in different socioeconomic status.

Consumer researchers have accumulated data that suggest the usefulness of the life-course approach to the study of the older adults' consumer behavior. For example, Lumpkin, Gibler, and Moschis (1992) found that many older adults do not identify the need for retirement housing until after a significant event—either a death, physical tragedy, or financial problem. The same study found that information acquisition and search patterns differ, depending on what triggered interest in retirement housing. Those reacting to a significant event tend to gather limited information and make a decision in as little as six weeks, while those taking a proactive approach to retirement may take up to six years to make a decision. However, only the study by Andreasen (1984) examined the effects of selected life events on consumer behavior. Specifically, the effects of 23 objective life status changes were assessed on specific changes in lifestyles and consumer behaviors such as brand differences using stress as an intervening variable.

Studying ways older people cope with transitions, events, and new life conditions can provide useful information for marketing strategy. Experiencing and anticipating events may create needs for products and services. For example, Schewe and Balazs (1992) discuss how transition into several roles may create needs for products and services. Similarly, Schewe and Meredith (1994) discuss marketing opportunities due to life-stage changes, citing a Yankelovich study which showed that 40% of households changing their address also changed their brand of toothpaste. In a similar vein, Krafft (1993) discusses how marketers of selected products and services target pre-movers who develop specific consumption needs in anticipation of relocation.

Marketers target their markets by focusing on consumers at different stages in life, or on those who have experienced or are about to experience events that mark transition into a new stage in life. Mergenhagen (1995) discusses several other important transitions that have implications for marketers. Transitions create needs for products and services. Many companies have begun to use consumer life transitions as a focus point in developing marketing strategy either by identifying and targeting consumers in transition or by offering refined products that are most suitable to specific needs. For example, Northwestern Mutual Life develops its product mix based on three major life stages: parenthood, pre-retirement, and maturity. In its brochure, "Life Stages and Life Needs," the company promotes different financial services to families at different life stages. Similarly, Fidelity Investments alerts its clients to major life events that are likely to alter their investment goals (and subsequent needs for different financial services). Ikea, a major furniture company, found through research that consumers make their purchasing decisions based on life changes (such as marriage, parenthood, and relocation). Another example can be seen in companies which are marketing a wide variety of products and services—from calcium, to hormone therapy, to exercise videos—to menopausal women. Menopause, a process that occurs at the average age of 51, is becoming a big business as more baby boomers are experiencing this life-stage change (Braus 1993). The transition into this new life stage is not limited to women but it also applies to men. As Cutler (1993) puts it: "While the experience of middle-aged women is popularly characterized by the physical changes of menopause, men's passage is most often celebrated as a trauma of epic proportions" (p. 49). Often known as "mid-life crisis," this stage marks the transition into a new stage, creating anxiety and stress because of one's aging. Marketers try to treat such social discomforts with products and services ranging from hair-replacement procedures to eyelid surgery. A new industry, which has been referred to as "men's midlife services" (Cutler 1993), appears to be emerging with the aging of the baby boomers.

In building our Life-Stage model, we relied heavily upon the adaptation perspective for several reasons. First, this perspective serves as a framework for integrating other disjoined theoretical perspectives as well as the multitheoretical models of cognition and socialization. Second, it focuses our attention on key events that may be crucial in affecting the older person's aging, raising two key questions: (1) what are the key events older adults are likely to experience? (2) how do these events affect aging and subsequent older consumers' responses to marketing variables of the firm? While research is available to answer the first question, the effects of specific events on aging and changing patterns of consumer behavior becomes a challenging task for our research efforts. Thus, we sought to identify key markers of life transitions and events to which the older person must adapt. Finally, the adaptation perspective is also useful in explaining recent research on cognition that suggests the potential for continuous improvement of existing skills and acquisition of compensatory skills and new cognitive skills throughout life, a phenomenon often referred to as *plasticity* of the cognitive system (Perlmutter 1988; Willis and Schaie 1988).

SUMMARY AND IMPLICATIONS FOR DEVELOPING A COMPREHENSIVE LIFE-STAGE MODEL

The information presented in this chapter suggests several guidelines for developing a comprehensive model to explain consumer behavior in later life.

1. Consumer behavior of older adults may be viewed as an outcome of biophysical, psychological, and social aging, as well as the result of interaction of these aging processes.

2. There are several explanations (theories) of these aging processes, with each explanation helping us understand specific aspects of the older person's behavior in the marketplace.

3. In order to adequately understand various aspects of the older person's consumer behavior, one must consider the wide variety of explanations offered. Therefore, factors used to construct explanatory models should derive from a wide variety of theoretical perspectives.

4. The factors that should be included in a comprehensive model of consumer behavior in later life do not affect all mature adults the same way; their influence varies by life stage, and they affect the individual's transition into a given stage.

5. While many life-stage transitions are often related to the aging processes (biophysical, psychological, and social), the movement is also influenced by the occurrence of recent life events. These life events should be considered in developing a comprehensive model because they affect consumer behavior directly or indirectly by influencing various aging processes.

Thus, in order to build a sound model of consumer behavior in later life, one must provide answers to questions such as: What aspects of consumer behavior are likely to change in later life? What are the available explanations (theories) that can help us understand such changes? How do we operationalize these theories and apply relevant factors derived from these perspectives to a com prehensive model? How do we test the derived model to assess its utility? How do we take into account the heterogeneity of the mature consumer market in developing an "all-inclusive" model? These questions, along with the guidelines suggested in this chapter, are addressed and used as a basis for developing the Life-Stage model. Specifically, the model recognizes the heterogeneity of the mature population by treating these consumers differently based on the "stages" in which they are located—expecting them to behave differently as market segments depending on their stage in life.

REFERENCES

Andreasen, Alan R. (1984). "Life Status Changes and Changes in Consumer Preferences and Satisfaction." *Journal of Consumer Research*, 11 (December): 784–794.

Atchley, Robert C. (1987). *Aging: Continuity and Change* (2nd ed.). Belmont, CA: Wadsworth Publishing Company.

———. (1989). "A Continuity Theory of Normal Aging." *The Gerontologist*, 29(2): 183–190.

Balkwell, Carolyn. (1985). "An Attitudinal Correlate of the Timing of a Major Life Event: The Case of Morale in Widowhood." *Family Relations* (October): 577–581.

Baltes, Paul, Hayne W. Reese, and Lewis P. Lipsitt. (1980). "Life-Span Developmental Psychology." *Annual Review of Psychology*, 31: 65–110.

Braus, Patricia. (1993). "Facing Menopause." *American Demographics* (March): 45–48.

Buhler, Charlotte. (1968). "The General Structure of the Human Life Cycle." In *The Course of Human Life*, eds. C. Buhler and F. Massarik. New York: Springer.

Burbank, Patricia M. (1986). "Psychosocial Theories of Aging: A Critical Evaluation." *Advances in Nursing Science*, 9(1) (October): 73–86.

Caspi, Avshalom, and Glen H. Elder, Jr. (1988). "Childhood Precursors of the Life Course." In *Childhood Development in Life Span Perspective*, eds. E. Mavis Hetherington, Richard M. Lerner, and Marion Perlmutter. Hillsdale, NJ: Lawrence Erlbaum Associates, pp. 115–142.

Clausen, John A. (1986). *The Life Course: A Sociological Perspective*. Englewood Cliffs, NJ: Prentice-Hall.

Cole, Catherine A., and Gary J. Gaeth. (1990). "Cognitive and Age-Related Differences in the Ability to Use Nutritional Information in a Complex Environment." *Journal of Marketing Research*, 27 (May): 175–184.

Cowgill, D. O. (1974). "Aging and Modernization: A Revision of the Theory." In *Late Life*, ed. J. F. Gubrium. Springfield, IL: Charles C. Thomas, pp. 123–146.

Cristofalo, Vincent J. (1988). "An Overview of the Theories of Biological Aging." In *Emergent Theories of Aging*, eds. James E. Birren and Vern Bengtson. New York: Springer, pp. 118–127.

Cutler, Blayne. (1993). "Marketing to Menopausal Men." *American Demographics* (March): 49.

Danigelis, Nicholas L., and Alfred P. Fengler. (1990). "Homesharing: How Social Exchange Helps Elders Live at Home." *The Gerontologist*, 30(2): 162–170.

Dannefer, Dale. (1988). "What's in a Name? An Account of the Neglect of Variability in the Study of Aging." In *Emerging Theories of Aging*, eds. James E. Birren and Vern L. Bengtson. New York: Springer Publishing Company, pp. 356–384.

Dean, Ward. (1988). *Biological Aging Measurement: Clinical Applications*. Los Angeles: Center for Bio-Gerontology.

Denhardt, K. B., and P. W. Jeffress. (1971). "Social Learning and Economic Behavior: The Process of Economic Socialization." *The American Journal of Sociology*, 30: 113–126.

Dodd, Yvonne. (1990). "Survey Finds Older Adults Want Social Involvement, Would Like More Education." *Maturity Market Perspectives* (July 8).

Dowd, James J. (1975). "Aging as Exchange: A Preface to Theory." *Journal of Gerontology*, 30 (September): 584–594.

———. (1987). "Ever Since Durkheim: The Socialization of Human Development." Unpublished paper, University of Georgia.

Dychtwald, Ken, and Joe Flower. (1989). *Age Wave*. New York: St. Martin's.

Elder, G. (1974). *Children of the Great Depression*. Chicago: University of Chicago Press.

Erikson, Erik H. (1959). "Identity and the Life Cycle." *Psychological Issues*, 1: 18–171.

———. (1963). *Childhood and Society*. New York: W. W. Norton.

Eysenck, H. J. (1983). "Stress, Disease and Personality: The Inoculation Effect." In *Stress Research*, ed. C. Cooper. New York: John Wiley, pp. 121–146.

Featherman, Davil L., and Richard M. Lerner. (1985). "Ontogenesis and Sociogenesis: Problematic for Theory and Research about Development and Socialization Across the Lifespan." *American Sociological Review*, 50 (October): 659–676.

Flavell, J. H. (1977). *Cognitive Development*. Englewood Cliffs, NJ: Prentice-Hall.

Fry, Christine L. (1988). "Theories of Age and Culture." In *Emergent Theories of Aging*, eds. James E. Birren and Vern L. Bengtson. New York: Springer, pp. 447–481.

Gaeth, Gary J., and Timothy B. Heath. (1987). "The Cognitive Processing of Misleading Advertising in Young and Old Adults: Assessment and Training." *Journal of Consumer Research*, 14 (June): 43–54.

Garfinkel, H. (1967). *Studies in Ethnomethodology*. New York: Praeger.

George, Linda K. (1982). "Models of Transitions in Middle and Later Life." *Annals of the Academy of Political and Social Science*, 464: 22–37.

Goslin, David A. (ed.). (1969). *Handbook of Socialization Theory and Research*. Chicago: Rand McNally.

Gubrium, J., and D. Buckholdt. (1977). *Toward Maturity*. San Francisco: Jossey-Bass.

Hagestad, Gunhild O., and Bernice L. Neugarten. (1985). "Age and the Life Course." In *Handbook of Aging and the Social Sciences* (2nd ed.), eds. R. Binstock and E. Shanas. New York: Van Nostrand Reinhold, pp. 35–61.

Harris, Richard J. (1986). "Recent Trends in the Relative Economic Status of Older Adults." *Journal of Gerontology*, 41(3): 401–407.

Henderson, S., D. G. Byrne, and P. Duncan-Jones. (1981). *Neurosis and the Social Environment*. Sydney: Academic Press.

Hendricks, J., and C. Hendricks. (1977). *Aging in Mass Society: Myths and Realities*. Cambridge, MA: Winthrop.

Herzog, Regula A., Bruce M. Brock, Nancy H. Fultz, Morton B. Brown, and Ananias

C. Diokno. (1988). "Urinary Incontinence and Psychological Distress Among Older Adults." *Psychology and Aging*, 3(2): 115–121.

Heslop, Louise, and Judith Marshall. (1991). "On Golden Pond: Elderly Couples and Decision Making." In *Advances in Consumer Research*, Vol. 18, eds. Rebecca Holman and Michael Solomon. Provo, UT: Association for Consumer Research, pp. 681–687.

Hughes, Dana C., Dan G. Blazer, and Linda K. George. (1988). "Age Differences in Life Events: A Multivariate Controlled Analysis." *International Journal of Aging and Human Development*, 27(3): 207–220.

Jache, Ann. (1986). "The Adult Children of Elderly Widows: The Consequences of Being Part of a Support Network for Adult Children's Socialization for Their Own Age." Unpublished doctoral dissertation, University of Notre Dame.

John, Deborah Roedder, and Catherine Cole. (1986). "Age Differences in Information Processing: Understanding Deficits in Young and Elderly Consumers." *Journal of Consumer Research*, 13 (December): 297–315.

Karp, David A. (1988). "A Decade of Reminders: Changing Age Consciousness Between Fifty and Sixty Years Old." *The Gerontologist*, 128(6): 727–738.

Kassarjian, Harold H., and Mary Jane Sheffet. (1991). "Personality and Consumer Behavior: An Update." In *Perspectives in Consumer Behavior*, eds. Harold H. Kassarjian and Thomas S. Robertson. Englewood Cliffs, NJ: Prentice-Hall, pp. 281–316.

Korzenny, F., and K. Neuendorf. (1980). "Television Viewing and Self-Concepts of the Elderly." *Journal of Communication*, 30(1) (Winter): 31–80. "Research." In *Aging in the 1980's*, ed. Leonard W. Poon. Washington, DC: American Psychological Association, pp. 542–551.

Krafft, Susan. (1993). "Reaching Movers Before the Big Day." *American Demographics* (December): 14.

Kuypers, J., and V. Bengtson. (1973). "Social Behavior and Competence: A Model of Normal Aging." *Human Development*, 3: 181–201.

Lerner, Richard M. (1988). "Personality Development: A Life-Span Perspective." In *Child Development in Life-Span Perspective*," eds. E. Mavis Hetherington, Richard M. Lerner, and Marion Perlmutter. Hillsdale, NJ: Lawrence Erlbaum Associates, pp. 21–46.

Letsou, Antigone P., and Leilani S. Price. (1987). "Health, Aging, and Nutrition." *Clinics in Geriatric Medicine*, 3(2) (November): 253–260.

Light, Leah L. (1988). "Language and Aging: Competence Versus Performance." In *Emergent Theories of Aging*, eds. James E. Birren and Vern L. Bengtson. New York: Springer, pp. 177–213.

Lumpkin, James R., Karen M. Gibler, and George P. Moschis. (1992). *Retirement Housing and Long-Term Health Care: Attitudes and Perceptions of the Mature Consumer*. Annapolis, MD: National Association of Senior Living Industries.

MacNeil, Richard D., and Michael L. Teague. (1987). *Aging and Leisure: Vitality in Later Life*. Englewood Cliffs, NJ: Prentice-Hall.

Martin, R. (1971). "The Concept of Power: A Critical Defense." *British Journal of Sociology*, 22: 240–257.

Mathur, Anil. (1991). "The Role of Care Providers in the Consumer Socialization of the Elderly." Unpublished doctoral dissertation, Georgia State University.

Mathur, Anil, Kelly Smith, and George P. Moschis. (1992). "The Elderly's Motivation for Charity Gift Giving: An Exchange Theory Perspective.'' In *AMA Winter Proceedings*. Chicago: American Marketing Association.

Mayer, K. U., and N. B. Tuma. (1990). ''Life Course Research and Event History Analysis: An Overview.'' In *Event History Analysis in Life Course Research*, eds. K. U. Mayer and N. B. Tuma. Madison: The University of Wisconsin Press, pp. 3–20.

McClearn, Gerald E. (1981). ''Evolution and Genetic Variability.'' In *Developmental Plasticity: Behavioral and Biological Aspects of Variations in Development*, ed. E. S. Golin. New York: Academic Press, pp. 3–31.

McLeod, Jack M., and Garrett O'Keefe, Jr. (1972). ''The Socialization Perspective and Communication Behavior.'' In *Current Perspectives in Mass Communication Research*, eds. Gerald Kline and P. Tichenor. Beverly Hills, CA: Sage, pp. 121–168.

Mergenhagen, Paula. (1995). *Targeting Transitions*. Ithaca, NY: American Demographics, Inc.

Moody, Harry R. (1988). ''Toward a Critical Gerontology: The Contribution of the Humanities to Theories of Aging.'' In *Emergent Theories of Aging*, eds. James E. Birren and Vern L. Bengtson. New York: Springer, pp. 19-40.

Moschis, George P. (1987). *Consumer Socialization: A Life-Cycle Perspective*. Boston: Lexington Books.

———. (1992). *Marketing to Older Consumers*. Westport, CT: Quorum Books.

———. (1994). *Marketing Strategies for the Mature Market*. Westport, CT: Quorum Books.

Moschis, George P., and Harash Sachdev. (1991). ''Age-Related Differences in Acceptance of Technological Innovations.'' Atlanta: Georgia State University, Center of Mature Consumer Studies.

Moschis, George P., Anil Mathur, and Ruth B. Smith. (1993). ''Older Consumers' Orientations Toward Age-Based Marketing Stimuli.'' *Journal of the Academy of Marketing Science*, 21(3): 193–205.

Murrell, Stanley A., Fran H. Norris, and Christopher Grote. (1988). ''Life Events in Older Adults.'' In *Life Events and Psychological Functioning*, ed. Lawrence H. Cohen. Newbury Park, CA: Sage Publications, pp. 96–122.

Mutran, Elizabeth, and Donald C. Reitzes. (1984). ''Intergenerational Support Activities and Well-Being among the Elderly: A Convergence of Exchange and Symbolic Interaction Perspectives.'' *American Sociological Review*, 49(1) (February): 117–130.

Natow, Annette, and Jo-Ann Heslin. (1980). *Geriatric Nutrition*. Boston: BI Publishing Company, Inc.

Neugarten, Bernice L. (1977). ''Personality and Aging.'' In *Handbook of the Psychology of Aging*. (2nd ed.), eds. James E. Birren and K. Warner Schaie. New York: Van Nostrand Reinhold, pp. 626–649.

O'Guinn, Thomas C., and Ronald J. Faber. (1991). ''Mass Communication.'' In *Handbook of Consumer Behavior Theory and Research*, eds. Harold Kassarjian and Thomas Robertson. Englewood Cliffs, NJ: Prentice-Hall, pp. 349–400.

Passuth, Patricia M., and Vern L. Bengtson. (1988). ''Sociological Theories of Aging: Current Perspectives and Future Directions.'' In *Emergent Theories of Aging*, eds. James E. Birren and Vern L. Bengtson. New York: Springer, pp. 333–355.

Perlmutter, Marion. (1988). ''Cognitive Potential Throughout Life.'' In *Emergent Theories of Aging*, eds. James E. Birren and Vern L. Bengtson. New York: Springer, pp. 247–268.

Phillips, Lynn W., and Brian Sternthal. (1977). "Age Differences in Information Processing: A Perspective on the Aged Consumer." *Journal of Marketing Research*, 14 (November): 444–457.

Piaget, Jean. (1983). "Piaget's Theory." In *Handbook of Child Psychology*, Vol. 4, ed. P. H. Mussen. New York: Wiley, pp. 103–128.

Pirki, James R., and Anna L. Babic. (1988). *Guidelines and Strategies for Designing Transgenerational Products*. Acton, MA: Copley Publishing Company.

Reker, Gary T., and Paul T. P. Wong. (1988). "Aging as an Individual Process: Toward a Theory of Personal Meaning." In *Emergent Theories of Aging*, eds. James E. Birren and Vern L. Bengtson. New York: Springer, pp. 214–246.

Riegel, Klaus F. (1976). "Toward a Dialectical Theory of Human Development." *Human Development*, 18: 50–64.

Riley, Matilda W., A. Foner, Beth Hess, and Marcia L. Toby. (1969). "Socialization for the Middle and Later Years." In *Handbook of Socialization Theory and Research*, ed. David Goslin. Chicago: Rand McNally.

Riley, Matilda W., Marilyn Johnson, and Anne Foner. (1972). *Aging and Society, Vol. 3: A Sociology of Age Stratification*. New York: Russell Sage Foundation.

Rodin, Judith, and Ellen Langer. (1980). "Aging Labels: The Decline of Control and the Fall of Self-Esteem." *The Journal of Social Issues*, 36(2) (Spring): 12–29.

Rose, Arnold M. (1965). "Group Consciousness Among the Aging." In *Older People and Their Social World*, eds. A. M. Rose and W. A. Peterson. Philadelphia: Davis.

Rosenberg, M. (1979). *Conceiving the Self*. New York: Basic Books.

Ryff, Carol D. (1982). "Successful Aging: A Developmental Approach." *The Gerontologist*, 22(2): 209–214.

Salthouse, Timothy A. (1985). *A Theory of Cognitive Aging*. Amsterdam: North Holland.

———. (1991). *Theoretical Perspectives on Cognitive Aging*. Hillsdale, NJ: Lawrence Erlbaum Associates.

Schaie, K. Warner. (1987). "Applications of Psychometric Intelligence to the Prediction of Everyday Competence in the Elderly." In *Cognitive Functioning and Social Structure Over the Life Course*, eds. Carmi Schooler and K. Warner Schaie. Norwood, NJ: Ablex, pp. 50–58.

Schewe, Charles D. (1988). "Marketing to Our Aging Population: Responding to Physiological Changes." *Journal of Consumer Marketing*, 15 (Summer): 61–73.

———. (1991). "Strategically Positioning Your Way Into the Aging Marketplace." *Business Horizons* (May-June): 59–66.

Schewe, Charles D., and Anne L. Balazs (1992). "Role Transitions in Older Adults: A Marketing Opportunity." *Psychology and Marketing*, 9 (March/April): 85–99.

Schewe, Charles D., and Geoffrey E. Meredith (1994). "Digging Deep to Delight the Older Consumer." *Marketing Management*, 3(3): 21–35.

Schutz, A. (1967). *The Phenomenology of Social World*. (Introduction by George Walsh.) Evanston, IL: Northwestern University Press.

Sherman, Susan R., Russell A. Ward, and Mark LaGory. (1985). "Socialization and Aging Group Consciousness: The Effects of Neighborhood Age Concentration." *Journal of Gerontology*, 40(1): 102–109.

Shock, N. W. (1977). "System Intergration." In *Handbook of the Biology of Aging*, eds. C. E. Finch and L. Hayflick. New York: Van Nostrand Reinhold, pp. 639–661.

Smedley, Lawrence T. (1975). "The Patterns of Early Retirement." *AFL-CIO American Federationist* (April).

Smith, Ruth B., and George P. Moschis. (1990). "The Socialization Approach to the Study of the Elderly Consumer." In *Review of Marketing*, ed. Valarie Zeithaml. Chicago: American Marketing Association, pp. 190–226.

Swank, Constance. (1979). "Media Uses and Gratifications." *American Behavioral Scientist*, 23(1) (September/October): 95–117.

Thomae, H. (1970). "Theory of Aging and Cognitive Theory of Personality." *Human Development*, 13: 1–16.

Vaillant, G. E. (1977). *Adaptation to Life*. Boston: Little, Brown and Company.

Wagner, Janet, and Sherman Hanna. (1983). "The Effectiveness of Family Life Cycle on Consumer Expenditure Research." *Journal of Consumer Research*, 10 (December): 281–291.

Wallace, Everett S., and Anil Mathur. (1990). "Saving Behavior of the Mature Consumer: An Exchange Perspective." In *American Marketing Association Proceedings*, eds. William Bearden et al. Chicago: American Marketing Association, pp. 88–92.

Whitbourne, Susan Krauss. (1985). *The Aging Body: Physiological Changes and Psychological Consequences*. New York: Springer Verlag.

Willis, Sherry, and K. Warner Schaie. (1988). "Gender Differences in Spatial Ability in Old Age: Longitudinal and Intervention Findings." *Sex Roles*, 18(3/4): 189–203.

Wood, Vivian. (1971). "Age-Appropriate Behavior for Older People." *The Gerontologist*, 11(4, Part 1): 74–78.

Yates, Eugene F. (1988). "The Dynamics of Aging and Time: How Physical Action Implies Social Action." In *Emergent Theories of Aging*, eds. James E. Birren and Vern L. Bengtson. New York: Springer, pp. 90–117.

CHAPTER 3

The Segmentation Model

The preceding chapter showed that older people exhibit very heterogeneous patterns of thoughts and actions as a result of the different aging processes and circumstances they experience in late life. This further justifies the need for viewing the mature market as a composite of several segments rather than treating it as one homogeneous market. Thus, the mature market can be conceived of as a composite of diverse groups of people who differ as a result of different biological, social, and psychological aging processes and other circumstances they have encountered in their lives.

While segmentation analysis of the mature market is usually based on a single factor such as age, the use of multiple factors appears to be a more viable approach for two main reasons. First, differences in consumer responses among older people are not likely to be the result of any specific factor. Changes or differences in behavior in late life are usually the manifestation of different types of aging processes. Because people age differently, and aging is inherently multidimensional, a wide variability in attitudes, behaviors, and abilities exists. People age biologically, psychologically, socially, and even spiritually, and these aging processes are manifested in differences in attitudes and behaviors even among people of the same age.

Second, the use of any single criterion for segmentation not only is unlikely to capture the wide variability among older people, but also may not be appropriate or the most viable criterion. For example, consider personality traits used by many psychographic or lifestyle segmentation models. Several decades of research by Neugarten, a noted gerontologist, produced findings suggesting that personality changes little after age 30 (Barrow and Smith 1983). This finding is also confirmed by a recent Yankelovich study for *Modern Maturity* magazine, which shows few differences in lifestyles between younger and older adults (Yankelovich, 1987). Thus, one does not expect to find variability in personality in late life, and therefore personality and lifestyles may not be sound bases for segmenting the mature market, since they have been weak predictors of consumer behavior in general (Novak and MacEvoy, 1990).

This section reviews main segmentation attempts, evaluates these efforts in the context of the available knowledge presented in the previous chapter, and, based on these analyses and research already presented, develops our Life-Stage segmentation model.

PREVIOUS SEGMENTATION ATTEMPTS

Previous efforts to segment the mature market fall into two categories: those that use demographics as bases for segmentation; and efforts that use lifestyles and other psychological characteristics such as attitudes, personality, and motives. This section reviews and evaluates several types of segmentation models that use various bases or criteria for segmenting the mature market.

Age-Based Segments

Most marketers have used very simplistic approaches to segment the mature market by relying on demographic characteristics, especially age. Age is perhaps the most common segmentation criterion. Based on age, marketers can classify adults over a certain age into any number of age brackets and label them accordingly, if they so wish. While the definition of the mature market and the number of market segments are arbitrary decisions, marketers often use age 55 as the low age boundary for the older consumer market, and subsegments which consist of brackets defined by increments of ten years: 55 to 64, 65 to 74, 75 to 84, and 85 and older. This segmentation model is consistent with the way the U.S. Census Bureau compiles and reports age information, helping practitioners estimate the size of age segments very accurately. The U.S. Census Bureau also labels the four age groups as the olders, elders, aged, and very old, respectively.

Besides its usefulness in estimating present and projected numbers of older adults in the age subsegments, the value of age as a predictor of market behavior and as a segmentation tool is questionable. Because it is not age per se but factors related to age that can explain behavior, chronological age loses much of its glamour as an explanatory factor. Although many explanatory factors relate to age, there is a great deal of variability across such factors within a given age group. For this reason, the behavior of individuals in a given age group may not differ significantly from those in the next group, diminishing the value of age as a segmentation tool.

Buying-Style Segments

Using data from a national probability sample collected by Axiom Market Research Bureau, Towle and Martin (1976) segmented older adults (65+) on the basis of personality characteristics. The resultant six segments were given a psychographic description and were cross-classified by selected buying characteristics to "develop" six buying-style segments. While this approach used a sound methodology, the resultant segments were empirically derived. As a result, it is not clear why a psychographic segment should define, explain, or predict a buying-style segment. This study, however, was the first of its kind and stimulated additional efforts in developing more comprehensive models.

Bartos's Lifestyle Segments

Rena Bartos (1980) groups older people (50+) into six segments based on how they adjust to changes in time, money, and health as they move through the life passages of empty nest, retirement, loss of a spouse, and ill health.

Active Affluents. The active affluents (40%) are still working and in relatively good health. They have limited time and significant income. Active affluents are healthy consumers with the largest majority (90%) of them under 65 years of age. This segment is expected to be a good market for financial planning programs, annuities and other investments, luxury travel, restaurants, and theaters. They value their free time, and they are willing to pay for convenience, service, and speed.

Active Retireds. This group comprises 15% of the 50-and-over market, usually those who took early retirement while they were still in good health. Individuals in this segment do not want to be singled out but to live among people of all ages. The percentage of active retireds who move out of their own region after they stop working (4%) is below the average (8%) for the average retired population. They take extended vacations, although they may not use luxury liners or planes.

The Homemakers. This group makes up about 20% of the 50-and-over women who are above poverty level and full-time homemakers. There is a wide diversity among women in this segment, ranging from more affluent and relatively younger whose husbands are active affluents to older, lesser educated, and economically not so well-off. Homemakers must make important adjustments when they experience "empty nest" and must see their husbands move from work to retirement. Wives of active affluents can often compensate for such changes by engaging in leisure activities with their husbands.

The remaining three groups are of little interest to marketers, according to Bartos. The *disadvantaged* (17%), those *in poor health* (less than 1%), and *others* (6%).

Bartos discusses how the three groups spend their money and time, and how they use the mass media as well as the types of products and services they buy. The predominant explanation offered is the amount of time and money available, health and stage in life cycle. Furthermore, it is not clear which aspects of consumer behavior are inferred from these lifestyles and which ones are empirically based.

"Adjustment to Old Age" Clusters

Another study used 200 gerontologists to estimate the sizes and characteristics of nine predetermined market segments of senior citizens based on previous research on how people adjust to late life. The gerontologists were questioned on how well a set of attitudes and behaviors described each cluster. Analysis of these responses revealed two dimensions (factors) which summarize the attitudes and behaviors of older adults and help better describe these nine groups: (1) the extent to which old age is viewed as another stage of life to be experienced and enjoyed; and (2) the degree of insecurity and dependence associated with the adjustment pattern. Thus, the nine groups can be "positioned" along these two dimensions based on the extent to which their members exhibit certain attitudes or behaviors related to these two factors (French and Fox 1985).

An advantage of this approach is that groupings are based on scientific grounds. In spite of its merit, however, this approach falls short of providing convincing evidence that the gerontologists' perceptions match those of older adults.

Attitudinal Segments

Morgan and Levy (1993) presented another segmentation model based on responses people gave to psychographic statements related to three specific types of products: travel, health, and food products. Although they claim to have used motivational research based on clinical psychology, the statements to which their subjects responded were basically product-specific psychographic statements, such as: "I am interested in products that would make my skin look younger." The researchers used the groups formed based on responses given to these statements to predict consumer behavior.

Because the model is based on questionable methodology, its usefulness is not clear. Motivation research, which is based on clinical psychology, does not rely on quantitative methods; therefore, it is not clear how the researchers have been able to reverse the tradition in motivation research, which relies exclusively on in-depth, qualitative interviews, into quantifiable attitudinal statements. Second, the product-specific attitudinal statements used cannot be very useful in predicting consumer behavior. For example, the "Nutrition Concerned" segment is the group most likely to be concerned with food additives. Thus, the researchers may tautologically define explanation for prediction. For example, those who are most likely to be concerned with food additives can also be labeled as "nutrition concerned," adding little value to the explanatory and predictive power of these derived segments. One is not sure whether specific behaviors the model predicts are not part of the set of the explanatory factors used to predict such behaviors.

Geromarket Attitudinal Groups

A study of 2,600 adults age 50 and over served as a basis for developing six geromarket attitudinal groups. The respondents were classified based on answers they gave to 94 psychographic or lifestyle statements, which were reduced to 25 factors (similarly answered, highly correlated responses). The six clusters were named based on the overriding tendency for a factor (psychographic) to be present in each group: Assureds (11%), Actives (11%), Sociables (17%), Contenteds (20%), Concerneds (18%), and Insecures (16%). The order of these clusters reflects each group's ability to cope with or manage two forces believed to dominate the older adults' life: external change (changes in the person's world), and internal change (changes in the older person). Thus, Assureds are better able to cope with life, while Insecures are less able to cope with life than any other group.

It is not clear how well these groups explain consumer behavior of older adults, or why people in each group are expected to behave in a different way than older adults in other groups. Furthermore, because this was a proprietary study (Goldring & Company 1987), the validity of the psychographic dimensions, their rationale, and the resultant groupings are not clear.

Lifestyles and Values of Older Adults (LAVOA)

LAVOA is a segmentation model developed by Stanford Research Institute (SRI) for the National Association for Senior Living Industries (NASLI). The study used to develop this model surveyed 3,600 individuals in a nationally representative sample of people 55 and older to identify four psychological factors that influence preferences for types of housing: (1) autonomy–independence (the extent to which people are driven by the need to be on their own); (2) introversion–extroversion (the degree to which people are outer-directed and seek social involvement); (3) self-indulgence–self-denial (the extent to which people seek gratification); and (4) resistance to change–openness to change (the degree to which people are adaptable). Using these four psychological factors as well as health status and socioeconomic factors, the study revealed six psychographic segments (Gollub and Javitz 1989).

Explorers. Explorers (22% of the older population) are introverted and self-reliant. They are in moderately better health, slightly younger and better educated than the average older person; and they have average household incomes.

Explorers are likely to sell their homes for cash, and less likely than any other segment to believe that cultural, recreational, convenience services, and health-care services are essential in a retirement housing complex.

Adapters. This segment (11%) consists of older adults who are likely to be the most extroverted and open to change. Adapters value social relationships and material possessions. They are relatively well-educated, healthy, and wealthy, and they are likely to seek gratification. Adapters are likely to be full-nesters. Although they like where they live, they tend to consider alternative housing options, such as moving to a condominium, as well as relocating to warmer climate. This group appreciates (more than others) the availability of recreational amenities, and is willing to purchase a housing unit and pay a monthly service fee for such services.

Pragmatists. Pragmatists (21%) also tend to be extroverted, relatively old, slightly less-educated, and healthier than the average older person. They are conservatists and conformists in their values, socially dependent, and self-indulgent. Pragmatists tend to live alone and have thought about moving to a nursing home, a housing facility for older people, or to receive help in caring for themselves. Facilities that provide security services, central dining, beauty parlors, travel services, and a post office are some of the housing features that are likely to appeal to this group.

Attainers. This segment (9%) of older adults consists of the ''youngest,'' most autonomous, healthy, wealthy, and self-indulgent individuals. They are rela-tively well-educated and open to change. Attainers are self-satisfiers, oriented toward getting what they want, and impulse oriented. Individuals in this group are most likely to own their homes and most likely to live with a spouse and with children at home. Attainers are the group most likely to have thought about moving to another state, to a smaller home, or to live in a better climate with fewer chores. They prefer to have access to cultural events, movie thea-ters, parks and colleges, as well as access to other recreational amenities such as golf and tennis.

Martyrs. Martyrs (26%) are likely to be introverted and resistant to change. This group is the most self-denying, the least healthy, and the least wealthy, and not so well-educated. Martyrs tend to be the segment most likely to live with their children and to find their homes hard to maintain. Individuals in this group are those most likely to have considered moving to an adult community close to shopping and health-care facilities.

Preservers. Individuals in this segment (11%) are the least healthy and least wealthy. They tend to resist change and look up to others for maintaining and enhancing their well-being. Preservers are highly need-driven. They are most likely to live alone, usually in apartments or older-adult high-rise buildings. They would move primarily to other older-adult housing, and they are most likely to feel that security, central dining, meal delivery, maid, maintenance, and other similar services are essential to a retirement community. Preservers are likely to have considered moving to a nursing home so that they may receive help with a number of activities of daily living.

The LAVOA model is considered to be a product-specific segmentation model for older adult housing. Its main advantage appears to be the incorporation of more than just psychological factors as bases for profiling older adults, and the belief that these factors may be more suitable for housing choices. While socio-economic and health factors appear to make sense as variables that could determine housing choices, the four psychological variables remain descriptive (data-driven). The model provides little or no explanation as to "why" certain psychological characteristics should relate to housing decisions, or why these and no other/additional characteristics would not be useful as well.

Psychographic Models

Two other models were developed based on psychographic factors. One model was developed based on psychographic statements representing eight life-style dimensions (Sorce, Tyler, and Loomis 1989). These dimensions reflected changes that aging brings about, including changes in family composition, health, financial status, and social and physical activities. These dimensions were condensed into five representative lifestyle components, which provided the basis for forming six lifestyle clusters: Self-Reliant, Quiet Introverts, Family-Orienteds, Active Retirees, Young and Insecures, and Solitaires. These groups differed very little on demographic characteristics, but they differed markedly on other lifestyle and attitudinal dimensions. However, it is not clear whether these lifestyle and attitudinal dimensions on which the segments differed are the consequence of the different responses given by those in different clusters or were used to derive the six clusters. Unfortunately, the study did not attempt to determine the extent to which these lifestyle clusters are useful predictors of various aspects of consumer behavior, and the results may not be generalized to the U.S. population because of the possible bias in the nonrandom sample of 418 older adults used.

The other model was developed by Fela (1978), who used psychographic variables to group 1,314 older adults age 65 and over. According to this model, three segments emerged (p. 2):

Traditionalists—Conservative in nature, traditionalists tend to (1) hold strong moral and religious beliefs; (2) resist rapid change; (3) avoid risk; and (4) revel in the past. As self-possessed homebodies, home and family activities play a dominant role. Although concerned with contemporary issues, traditionalists are passive participants. Community work is not actively pursued by the group.

Outgoers—As community-concerned individuals, outgoers exhibit strong philanthropic tendencies. Consistent with this benevolent attitude, ecological considerations are strongly advocated. As a socially active group, they (1) travel extensively; (2) participate in club activities; and (3) support culturally oriented functions. Despite their strong traditional moral convictions, a less conservative attitude emanates.

Isolationists—An indifferent, withdrawn attitude permeates the isolationists' personality. Exemplifying this theme is their (1) noted detachment from clubs, social gatherings, and community work, and (2) blatant disregard of essential ecological imperatives. Attributed partly to their detachment from society, much unhappiness exists within this group. Moreover, despite their religious inclination, materialistic overtones emanate.

Other Lifestyle and Psychographic Models

There are several other lifestyle and psychographic models that were developed by commercial firms. Unfortunately, there is relatively little information on these models, the methodologies used to develop them, and their efficacy in predicting consumer behavior. As a result, their value and their relative desirability remains uncertain.

One such model was developed by Langer (1981). This model uses a number of attitudinal and lifestyle factors to develop a three-way division of the 50-plus age group: "*The Vitally Active*, who are busy, involved in the world, making discoveries, and experiencing a sense of life expanding. *The Adapters*, who have significant objective difficulties (limited fixed incomes, health problems) but who have learned to accept and overcome them. *The Overwhelmed*, who feel at a loss, adrift, unable to cope with their problems, and anxieties about the future" (p. 15).

Grey Advertising segmented the 55-plus group into equal-sized groups of Master Consumers, Maintainers, and Simplifiers. *Master Consumers* tend to be younger and better educated, and they possess nearly half (46%) of the buying power of the 50-plus population. They are secure and fulfilled and they look forward to their retirement, which they see as a time of pleasure—a time to do all the rewarding things they have put off in the past. *Maintainers* are also healthy and financially well-off, accounting for one-third of the 50-plus market's spending power. These individuals are not as active as they could be. They lack a sense of purpose that can guide them through their retirement years; and although they do not want to become rocking-chair grandpas or frumpy grandmas, they have no clear vision of themselves in post-retirement years. Finally, *Simplifiers* represent the stereotypical frail, inactive, and less-affluent older people, controlling just one-fifth of this market's buying power. These groups were developed based on personal interviews with a national probability sample of some 260 adults living in metro areas. Thus, due to the relatively small size of the sample used and its nonrepresentativeness, it would be dangerous to see these groups as an accurate portrayal of the 50-plus market (Grey Advertising 1988).

Finally, there are "lifestyle" segments which rely exclusively on age or stages in one's life cycle. For example, J. Walter Thompson's *Lifestages* is a system of demographic groups, although it is not clear how certain demographic characteristics relate to the demographic groups. The model relates attitudes, consumption, and media habits to each group. Similarly, Donnelley identifies the *Reward Driven* group (ages 50–64), the *Stability Driven* (ages 65–74), and the *Security Minded* (75+), while geodemographic models (such as those by Claritas and Age Connect) assume that the categories formed on the basis of demographic characteristics also share similar lifestyles.

Assessment of Psychographics and Lifestyles

Analysis of lifestyle and psychographic-based segments are useful in that they help us understand not only how older adults spend their money and time, but also provide generalized patterns of values, activities, and interests. More important, however, is the assumption that lifestyles and psychographics explain consumer behavior of older adults. The lifestyle models presented here are based on three different types of factors: sociodemographic characteristics, psychological (personality) factors, and psychographic characteristics. The last category includes patterns of activities, attitudes and values, and sometimes health status.

Bartos's model is based on sociodemographic characteristics, while the models of "buying styles," "adjustment to old age," and "geromarket" are based on personality factors. The two psychographic models are based on psychographic factors, while LAVOA uses a combination of sociodemographic, personality, and lifestyle factors. While these models are useful in helping us classify older adults and describe them as groups, their value in understanding the behavior of older adults is questionable. For example, while some demographic characteristics may help us understand some aspects of consumer behavior of older adults, demographic factors have not been very strong determinants of consumer behavior in general. The same can be said about personality and psychographics. Personality characteristics are weak correlates of consumer behavior. Similarly, psychographics account for an average of 2–3% of the variability in consumer behavior in general (Novak and MacEvoy 1990). Since personality and psychographics of younger adults show few differences from those of older adults (Yankelovich 1987), one must question the value of these factors in explaining consumer behavior of older adults.

Perhaps the most serious drawback of all previous methods, both published and proprietary, is that they cannot convince marketers of their value because they cannot demonstrate, using some objective criterion, that they are better than other methods. Researchers who develop a model simply do not compare the model's predictive ability to existing segmentation models. By failing to do so, researchers add to the long list of segmentation alternatives available to practitioners, but fail to help one choose the most appropriate segmentation model.

While development of lifestyles of the mature market is usually based on one single type of factor, such as sociodemographic or psychographic factors, the use of multiple factors appears to be a more viable approach to understanding behavior in late life. First, differences in consumer responses among older people are not likely to be the result of any specific factor. Changes or differences in behavior in late life are usually the manifestation of different types of aging processes. Because people age differently, and aging is inherently multidimensional, a wide variability in attitudes, behaviors, and abilities exists. People age biologically, psychologically, socially, and even spiritually, and these aging processes are manifested in differences in attitudes and behaviors even among people of the same age.

Second, the use of any single criterion or basis for grouping older adults is not only unlikely to capture the wide variability in such processes, but also may not be the most appropriate or the most viable criterion. For example, personality does not adequately capture psychological aging of the individual, and other psychological factors such as cognitive or subjective age (how old a person feels/thinks he or she is) might prove more effective than personality.

Finally, we must accept and use knowledge accumulated over several decades in the consumer field. This type of information suggests that consumer responses cannot simply be attributed to one single factor based on one set of assumptions. Rather, practitioners must consider information from several disciplines and base their decisions on such disciplinary contributions.

While lifestyle studies have been done for over 30 years, any lifestyle study that claims to predict consumer behavior or provide useful insights into motivations for consumption must be viewed with great suspicion. Not only do lifestyles represent a limited perspective on consumer behavior (one of several explanations), but the results of empirical studies show that these models are not powerful enough to warrant consideration as marketing tools.

GERONTOGRAPHICS

''Gerontographics'' (author's term) is an approach that acknowledges individual differences in aging processes as well as differences in type of aging dimensions that occur in late life. It attempts to gain insight into human behavior in late life by recognizing the multifaceted aspects of the aging process, and it considers consumer behavior to be a manifestation of these multidimensional processes and circumstances older people experience. Gerontographics is based on the premise that the observed similarities and differences in the consumer behavior of older adults is the outcome of several social, psychological, biophysical, life-time events, and other environmental factors, all affecting the aged person differently. The derivation of mature market subsegments is based on the premise that those older people who experience similar circumstances in late life (defined by the person's gerontographic characteristics) are likely to exhibit similar patterns of consumer behavior—patterns that differ from those of other older adults experiencing different sets of circumstances, that is, having different gerontographic characteristics.

Gerontographics is an approach similar to psychographics or lifestyles, but it focuses exclusively, and in much greater detail, on older adults' needs, attitudes, lifestyles, and behaviors. It differs from psychographics in a number of ways. First, gerontographics is a more comprehensive approach in that it considers the multiplicity of dimensions relevant to aging in late life. Besides psychological factors, which are the core bases in present lifestyle models (e.g., VALS 2, LOV), it also considers factors associated with biological aging as well as social and experiential aging. Second, the approach takes into consideration various external circumstances or events in late life that can produce variability in older adults' behavior. Third, the number of subgroupings (segments) and their corresponding names are derived or specified on an *a priori* basis, based on our knowledge about human behavior in late life. By contrast, models based on psychographics and lifestyles normally derive a segment after the data have been gathered, and the number and names of subgroupings are likely to differ across researchers or studies. For example, studies using psychographics and personality have yielded different conclusions about the numbers and names of subgroupings of the aged market, although they used similar methods (Goldring & Company 1987; Gollub and Javitz 1989). The marketer still must decide whether psychographics is a viable approach, and which psychographics or lifestyle model is best and why (Bernstein 1978).

Gerontographics, as an approach to market segmentation, seeks improvement over other approaches in three ways: (1) by acknowledging the scientifically based claim in a large number of disciplines (e.g., social gerontology) that no single theory or type of variable can adequately explain behavior in late life— that is, similarities and differences of the mature market; (2) by offering an explanation of why there should be a specific number of subsegments, as well as why older individuals in these groupings behave differently; and (3) by demonstrating that the derived segmentation model is more useful to marketers than are models based on limited types of variables.

DEVELOPMENT OF THE LIFE-STAGE MODEL

Age is often advocated as a key variable in defining life stages or times when transition into a new stage in life is likely to occur (Pol, May, and Hartranft 1992). Perhaps the reason for emphasis on age, even among those who admit wide variation in aging across individuals, is due to its simplicity and data availability. Other variables such as health can also be used as markers of life-stage transitions, but health should be assessed objectively, not subjectively. Because the body has the ability to adapt to its environment, one finds little variability in self-reported health over the life span (based on the results reported by the National Center for Health Statistics based on National Health Interview Surveys); with age, people continue to report they are in relatively good health, despite their increasing use of medications for ailments and chronic conditions. Because of the wide variability in aging across individuals, age is not a useful variable to consider in defining life stages. For example, women experience menopause in their thirties, forties, fifties, and even in their sixties. Thus, the need for products and services that are likely to be demanded due to such changes in the reproductive system may also show a wide variability.

Preliminary Steps

In developing a comprehensive model of older consumer behavior, it was necessary to take a number of steps. First, a state-of-the-art review of the available literature on aging and behavioral studies on the aged was conducted. This task included several on-line searches on published documents, analysis of data available from proprietary studies and reports, and examination of trade and media writeups. This step was necessary in order to develop an understanding of the processes that characterize aging, and the changes that may occur as a result of the person's adaptation to changing life conditions (see Chapter 2). This task was also necessary in order to uncover factors identified in previous studies of older people that relate to various aspects of their consumer behavior.

Second, the compilation of the available literature pointed to two broad types of information: one concerned the theoretical and conceptual foundations of human behavior in later life; and the second focused on the factors that affect consumer behavior in later life as revealed from empirical studies. We tried to integrate these two types of information by (1) seeking consumer-behavior findings that could be interpreted in the context of a specific theory, and (2) evaluating each finding from the consumer field in the context of relevant theories. This theory-and-data interplay was necessary in order to identify viable theories from other fields that would be helpful in the consumer area, and in order to eliminate spurious data in the consumer field that could not be interpreted or understood in the context of theory. Furthermore, the aspects of consumer behavior that were analyzed or interpreted in line with theory were confined to behaviors that could be influenced by the marketer. These included preferences for (and consumption of) products and services, and specific attributes such as packaging, labeling, brands, and warranties; promotions such as advertising content, senior discounts, and senior programs; pricing such as "cents-off," "sales," and multiple-pricing; and preferences for specific store services. In sum, this process was designed to uncover theory-driven and marketing-action-oriented consumer behaviors. The information that was compiled had to meet the following two requirements: (1) differences in older consumer behavior on marketing-driven variables had to be present; and (2) one or more explanations of, or justification for, the observed differences had been offered. Anecdotal evidence from trade publications and mass media were used to supplement or even replace the first requirement when empirical data were lacking.

Based on data related to the second requirement, a number of assumptions and hypotheses were developed. These concerned specific theory-based factors that affect specific aspects of consumer behavior that can be influenced by marketers. For example, biological declines were assumed to create needs for specific products and services, cognitive deficits were expected to lead to preferences for information-presentation formats, and loss of spouse was hypothesized to increase the need for learning tasks that used to be performed by the deceased spouse. Several hundred assumptions and hypotheses were developed, and some additional examples are given in our previous work (Moschis 1994).

Qualitative and Interpretive Work

One of the goals of science is to help us explain a phenomenon, and a prerequisite to explanation is understanding. Qualitative and interpretive work is useful in this regard, and has been increasingly gaining acceptance among consumer researchers in the process of scientific discovery. Nonempirical or ''humanistic'' approaches are also advocated as useful means of complementing empirical data. We employed these methods, which consisted of various types of introspective formats such as brain-writing, synectics, focus groups, and analyses of case studies.

We used qualitative and interpretive analyses in order to accomplish two major types of goals. First, we attempted to identify and validate aging processes or themes that relate to consumer behavior, uncover additional themes or processes that have implications for consumer behavior in later life, and interpret data in the context of existing theories of aging. These processes provided stronger support for their relevance to the study of older consumer behavior, helping us understand older consumer perceptions, needs, and meanings of some products and marketing stimuli. Second, we sought to determine typologies of older consumers on the basis of their responses to theory-driven variables of the firm. The latter task was necessary for determining the number of older consumer groups on an *a priori* bases, before empirical validation; it also was the most challenging one.

These humanistic methods were useful in identifying and validating the three aging processes that may relate to consumer behavior. For example, participants of focus groups made comments about their vision problems and difficulty in reading fine print, and how retirement and widowhood affected their consumption needs. Once these aging themes were identified for the relevance to the consumer behavior of older people, we used interpretive work and sought to establish the possible number of types of older consumers in the context of the three aging processes. Theoretically, it was expected that older consumers had to fall into a minimum of two groups—those who had not experienced any of the aging processes, and those who had experienced the three aging processes, assuming that these processes are interrelated and each occurs dialectically and in a relatively short time. We also made the assumption that these processes, although interdependent, may occur over a relatively long time, creating the possibility that one may have experienced any combination of the three aging processes. This assumption created eight possible combinations, suggesting that there might be as many as eight different types of older consumers, as shown below.

Older Consumer Typology	Biophysical	Types of Aging Experienced Psychological	Social
1	no	no	no
2	yes	no	no
3	yes	yes	no
4	yes	yes	yes
5	no	yes	yes
6	no	no	yes
7	no	yes	no
8	yes	no	yes

A main issue in considering this typology is whether transitions or changes in biological, psychological, and social states occur over a significant length of time, which would allow one to observe older consumers in transition. Another related issue is whether some of these changes occur more closely together or simultaneously, which would not allow people to be "located" in the various classes or categories. Other relevant issues addressed were: What are the key life changes and role transitions that have implications for aging? What social, psychological, and biological events serve as markers of transition and change affecting components of the aging processes? What types of adjustment or adaptation have implications for consumer behavior changes and marketing strategy? Should one use objective or subjective measures of biophysical, psychological, and social aging?

The available literature reviewed suggested that biophysical aging is a gradual process, and psychological aging takes place over a much longer time than transitions to new roles and, therefore, social aging (e.g., grandparenthood). The fact that older people hold onto the self-image they developed in earlier life suggests a significant time lag between biological and psychological aging. Similarly, the relationship between biological and social aging may also be asynchronous, as in the case of a retiree who is in excellent health, or early-life grandparenthood. Such social-role transitions are not likely to affect biological aging, but most likely they would affect the person's psychological aging due to adaptation to new social roles. On the other hand, the relationship between social and psychological aging is expected to be stronger, and people may respond psychologically to social aging promptly, as in the case of retirement, where psychological preparation begins 10 to 15 years in advance. Thus, we reasoned that to the extent psychological and social aging are closely interrelated, the eight possible categories would be reduced to four, which would classify older adults based on the biophysical and psychosocial dimensions. Finally, we concluded that subjective measures may be inadequate in capturing aging, since aging (especially biological) involves gradual processes of change; they need to be supplemented with objective measures of key events, conditions, circumstances, and life transitions. The term ''gerontographics'' was used to capture the physical, psychological, and social changes and consequences of aging.

Surveys

A series of studies conducted by researchers at the Center for Mature Consumer Studies (CMCS) used gerontographics—that is, variables that tap the person's biophysical, psychological, and social states in life, as well as key life events that are likely to contribute to the older person's aging processes (via stress disorder and role transitions—see Chapter 2) to produce the Life-Stage model, which consists of four groups of older adults who are at four different stages in late life (see Figure 3.1). The first stage includes *healthy indulgers*. Mature Americans who are at this stage are closest to the stage most baby boomers are found. The major difference between mature people who experience this stage and baby boomers is that the former group is better off financially and settled career-wise, with their main focus on enjoying life rather than trying to ''make it in life.'' Opposite to this stage is the life stage occupied by *frail recluses*, or people with chronic ailments who are mostly in isolation and are likely to think of themselves as ''old persons.'' At some earlier point in time, they may have experienced the same stage healthy indulgers presently do, although stages are age-irrelevant. Many of the frail recluses may have gone through the intermediate life stages experienced by *healthy hermits* and *ailing outgoers*. The former group is relatively more socially withdrawn and healthy but secluded, while the latter is still active and likely to maintain high self-esteem despite health problems. Furthermore, healthy hermits are concerned with day-to-day tasks and likely to deny their ''old age'' status, while ailing outgoers have internalized many of their frailties; and, while they try to make the best out of life, ailing outgoers are preoccupied with their physical and financial independence and well-being. Thus, people in late life can move from one stage to another. Although such changes may occur over time and may be abrupt (e.g., retirement, stroke), the processes or ''flows'' are relatively age-irrelevant because they may begin at any age in later life, or may never be experienced.

While there are no age differences across the four segments, these groups differ across several domains that define life stages. *Healthy indulgers* have experienced the fewest life events (e.g., retirement, widowhood, chronic conditions) that may contribute to the person's psychological and social aging. As a result, they are the group most likely to behave like younger consumers. *Healthy hermits* are likely to have experienced life events (e.g., death of spouse) that have affected their self-concept and self-worth, and have forced them into psychological and social withdrawal. Many of them resent the fact that they have been forced into isolation and are expected to behave like old people. On the other hand, *ailing outgoers* is the group most likely to maintain positive self-esteem and self-concept, despite life events that demand changes in their

Figure 3.1
Life-Stage Segments of the Mature Market

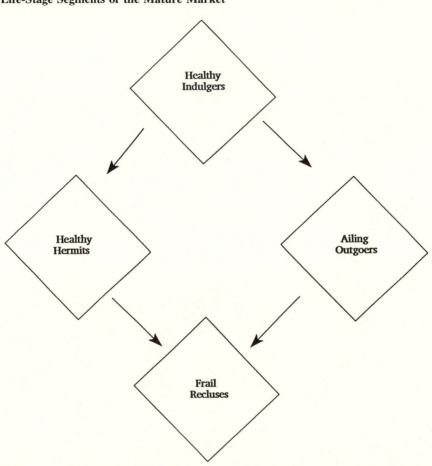

Note: Specific arrows indicate that people may move to the next stage in life due to physiological, psychological, and social aging. Arrows pointing to the left denote psychosocial aging; arrows pointing to the right denote biophysical aging.

lifestyles such as retirement, death of spouse, and health problems. Unlike healthy hermits, many ailing outgoers accept the ''old age'' status but refuse to change their lifestyle, acknowledging their limitations but still interested in getting the most out of life. Finally, *frail recluses* are likely to have accepted their older age status and have adjusted their lifestyles to reflect biophysical declines and changes in social roles. In order to cope with these detrimental changes in late life, they have become spiritually stronger. (The reader can consult Appendix B for more details on group profiles.)

While only a few factors are used here to describe the life-stage model, it is based on several dozen variables that have been found to affect behaviors and attitudes in late life. The model acknowledges individual differences in aging processes as well as differences in types of aging that occur in late life. It attempts to gain insight into human behavior in late life by recognizing the multifaceted aspects of the aging process, and considers consumer behavior to be a manifestation of these multidimensional processes and circumstances people experience in late life—that is, the person's gerontographic characteristics.

The empirical validation of this multifaceted, gerontographics-based life-stage segmentation model is based on three years of mail-questionnaire-survey responses from more than 3000 older consumers. Although the size of each market segment varies somewhat across surveys, deviations are within acceptable tolerance levels.

The modeling process began with a list of 136 behavioral variables cited in previous studies of the elderly. They ranged across several psychological, social, physiological, and experiential dimensions that relate to aging, as well as several structural factors and events that describe the older person's social position and life circumstances. Factor analysis derived composite variables, tapping the aging processes. These, along with several other variables, were subjected to cluster analysis to identify the different segments.

The four life stages were not only suggested by research in the field of aging and social sciences, but were also confirmed as better predictors of marketplace behavior. When they were compared to segments based on age, cognitive age, and psychographics (all of which tend to capture single dimensions of aging), older adults in the four life stages gave significantly more different responses to a large number of marketing offerings and strategies. For example, a study conducted by the author for AARP Andrus Foundation found that nearly twice as many ailing outgoers as healthy hermits (61.4% versus 33.7%) would use a medical ID card that can be electronically read by medical staff in case of emergency to show them useful health information. Healthy indulgers were twice as likely as frail recluses (21.3% versus 11.5%) to prefer directories of numbers that can be dialed for prerecorded information on various topics. In the same study, preferences did not differ by age for the two products. Two-thirds of ailing outgoers said they would like to see companies offering more senior discounts, compared to just 40% of healthy hermits. Again, there were no age differences in responses to senior discounts.

Researchers tested the model's ability to predict older adults' responses to several dozen marketing stimuli such as new products, advertising messages, sales promotions, price reductions, and various types of services. The model predicted responses twice as accurately as segments based on chronological or cognitive age groups. It also accounted for behavioral differences twice as well as previously published studies based on the Values and Lifestyle Segmentation (VALS) model developed by SRI.

In summary, the Life-Stage model is based on the premise that the observed similarities and differences in the consumer behavior of older adults is the outcome of several social, psychological, biophysical, lifetime events, and other environmental factors, that is, a person's gerontographics, all affecting the aged person differently. The derivation of mature market subsegments is based on the premise that those older people who have experienced similar circumstances in late life are likely to exhibit similar patterns of consumer behavior—patterns that differ from those of other older adults who have experienced a different set of circumstances.

Continuous Efforts

Our effort to understand older consumer behavior has (and always will be) continuous because consumers and the marketplace constantly change, and new research insights are developed every day that can help us improve our model. We began our empirical work with two large-scale surveys. One was a national probability survey of 1,469 adults aged 18 or over, of whom 961 were 55 or older. The purpose of this 1988 survey was to develop, validate, and test some of the assumptions about the Life-Stage groups. Marketing-related consumer behavior variables were applicable to a large number of marketing activities of the firm. This survey was supplemented with a regional survey one year later, consisting of 1,075 adults, of whom 709 were age 55 or older. The main purpose of this survey was to (1) test the validity and reliability of the original model developed on the basis of the national sample—to determine the extent to which the model applies to select geographic areas, and (2) to obtain information on older consumers' response to marketing variables of firms in various types of industries. Because our intent was not in estimating parameters (i.e., to represent the U.S. older consumer population) but rather in determining the extent to which different life-stage or gerontographic groups respond differently to marketing variables of different *types* of organizations, a national sample of older consumers was not deemed necessary. Both surveys used similar measures of aging processes as input into factor analysis and cluster analysis programs, and both surveys produced almost identical sizes of the four life-stage groups.

These efforts, as mentioned earlier, have been continuous and stem from the commonly held belief among scientists in various fields that the relationship between theory or method data is necessarily dialectic—that is, theory/method suggests data requirements, and data or findings help modify or recast theory and method. In this context, the model has the flexibility to incorporate additional variables that would enhance its explanatory and predictive ability, as our understanding about this consumer segment improves, market conditions change, and the present older consumers are replaced by new cohorts of aging Americans. Thus, the model maintains the features of being dynamic and flexible. We feel these are important features of the model, since researchers who have attempted to develop consumer groups in the past (e.g., VALS) have recognized the need to update their original model years later. Our recent work, for example, has been focusing on select life events that have implications for consumer behavior. As we add these life events to the existing list of variables that form the bases for our Life-Stage model, the model's explanatory ability can be assessed to determine the extent to which these new factors make a difference in our ability to predict the consumer behavior of the four life-stage groups.

PRODUCT/SERVICE-SPECIFIC RESPONSES

It should be emphasized that older consumers' responses to various types of marketing stimuli and strategies are likely to vary across products and services. Such responses tend to reflect the needs, attitudes, and lifestyles of each segment. In this section, we present examples of product/service-specific responses to several types of marketing offerings and activities of the firm—specifically, responses to products, information used or demanded, store attributes, and advertising.

Preferences for Products and Services

The author has surveyed elderly adults about their activities and preferences in a number of product categories, and has reported examples of intersegment differences found in his research (Moschis and Mathur 1993). For instance, proportionally twice as many ailing outgoers claim a preference for "how-to" educational materials than frail recluses. Similar patterns also apply to the popularity of adult education and do-it-yourself hobbies. The four segments also differ in their preferences for specific food-related services. When health becomes an important issue, as in the choice of dietary programs and prescriptions, a greater percentage of ailing outgoers favor them, compared to frail recluses and healthy hermits. Meanwhile, healthy indulgers favor fast-food home delivery more than other groups, particularly the frail recluses.

Research also reveals that among all elderly consumers, some marketing strategies and tactics are more appropriate than others, depending on the industry and on the segment. The patterns of behavior and attitude similarities and disparities among frail recluses, healthy hermits, ailing outgoers, and healthy indulgers will differ by industry, product, and service according to the needs, attitudes, and lifestyle of each segment (Moschis and Mathur 1993).

Information Needs

The groups that want to maintain their active lifestyles—healthy indulgers and ailing outgoers—express a greater need for information on health-related issues, as shown in their propensity to read newspaper and magazine ads that contain large amounts of updated information on health. On the other hand, the four groups do not differ much in their preferences for the same types of sources for food/beverage and fast-food products because such products in general are not as sensitive to aging processes in later life. However, when preferences for specific food products sensitive to some aging domains (e.g., health) are considered, the four groups are also likely to differ, with a higher percentage of ailing outgoers (47.8%) preferring dietary programs or dietary meals than frail recluses (32.8%) and healthy hermits (31.7%).

Patronage Motives

Specific reasons for buying a product or service also differ across both segments and industry. For example, the groups most likely to be socially and psychologically withdrawn—healthy hermits and frail recluses—are also likely to have fewer discretionary consumption needs than the more active groups. Thus, for a discretionary purchase such as a travel package, the importance of patronage motives such as price, selection, recommendations, and past satisfaction with vendors differs across the four groups (Moschis and Mathur 1993). The most active group—healthy indulgers—considers those factors the most.

Specific patronage motives differ not only across segments but also across types of products or services purchased, with such differences reflecting the aging dimensions describing each group. For example, the groups most likely to be socially and psychologically withdrawn (healthy hermits and frail recluses) are also likely to have fewer consumption needs, especially for discretionary consumption than the more active groups. Thus, for a discretionary purchase such as travel packages, patronage motives such as price, selection, advice of others, and past satisfaction with travel-package vendors differ across the four groups, with the most active group (healthy indulgers) considering these factors the most. However, for consumption of nondiscretionary (necessity) products such as food items, patronage motives are not as sensitive to the underlying dimensions that characterize older people in the four life stages. Older people tend to patronize food stores as frequently as younger people and, therefore, are equally active in their shopping for such products.

Industry Perceptions

Gerontographic groups also exhibit varying perceptions of different industries' images. For example, agreement across segments that "they rip off customers" is relatively uniform for insurance companies, and less so for travel-package vendors (Moschis and Mathur 1993).

Advertising Perceptions

Gerontographic factors also influence how mature consumers perceive advertising for different products and services. For example, healthy indulgers have the most favorable attitudes toward hospital and clinic television advertising, but the least favorable attitudes toward food and grocery store television ads, while ailing outgoers show the most favorable reaction (Moschis and Mathur 1993). The same research suggested additional observations that can be made with respect to a number of other marketing factors, such as responses to ads of products targeted primarily at older people. For example, because older people are much heavier consumers of drugs than younger adults, people in the four segments may be more sensitive to age stereotypes and to the age of the spokesperson in the ads. Thus, older adults most likely to notice the age of the spokespersons in pharmacy store ads are those most likely to be the heaviest consumers of drugs (ailing outgoers and frail recluses). However, for products or services such as travel, whose demand is fairly uniform across age groups, there are no significant group differences in perceptions of ads appealing to any specific age group, suggesting that older and younger persons may be equally used as spokespersons.

To summarize, marketers of products and services should be aware that the Life-Stage model may fit some products better than others. Findings derived from analysis of consumer responses to marketing factors in one industry would not apply to other industries, suggesting the need for industry-specific gerontographic segmentation and marketing-response models for greater effectiveness. When using gerontographic data, marketers must be sure to use information specific to their product or service category. Gerontographics is particularly useful in guiding marketing decisions in specific product categories because some of the groups are more sensitive to certain company offerings than other groups.

REFERENCES

Barrow, George M., and Patricia A. Smith. (1983). *Aging, The Individual and Society*. St. Paul, MN: West Publishing Company.

Bartos, Rena. (1980). "Over 49: The Invisible Consumer Market." *Harvard Business Review*, 58 (January-February): 140–148.

Bernstein, Peter. (1978). "Psychographics Still An Issue on Madison Avenue." *Fortune* (January 16): 78–84.

Fela, Leonard J. (1978). "The Elderly Consumer Market: A Psychographic Segmentation Study." *Dissertation Abstracts International*, 38(2A) (August): 1069–1070.

French, Warren A., and Richard Fox. (1985). "Segmenting the Senior Citizen Market." *Journal of Consumer Marketing*, 2(1) (Winter): 61–74.

Goldring & Company. (1987). *Geromarket Study*. Chicago: Goldring & Company.

Gollub, James, and Harold Javitz. (1989). "Six Ways to Age." *American Demographics*, 11 (June): 28–30, 35, 56.

Grey Advertising, Inc. (1988). *The Who and How-to of the Nifty 50-Plus Market*. New York: Grey Matter Editorial Board, Grey Advertising.

Langer, Judith K. (1981). *The 50 Plus Market: Who Says I'm Old?* New York: Judith Langer Associates.

Morgan, Carol, and Doran Levy. (1993). *Segmenting the Mature Market*. Chicago: Probus.

Moschis, George P. (1994). *Marketing Strategies for the Mature Market*. Westport, CT: Quorum Books.

Moschis, George P., and Anil Mathur. (1993). "How They Are Acting Their Age." *Marketing Management*, 2(2): 39–50.

Novak, Thomas P., and Bruce MacEvoy. (1990). "On Comparing Alternative Segmentation Schemes: The List of Values (LOV) and Values and Lifestyles (VALS)." *Journal of Consumer Research*, 7 (June): 105–109.

Pol, Louis G., Michael G. May, and Frank R. Hartranft. (1992). "Eight Stages of Aging." *American Demographics* (August): 54–57.

Sorce, Patricia, Philip R. Tyler, and Lynette M. Loomis. (1989). "Life Styles of Older Americans." *Journal of Consumer Marketing*, 6(3) (Summer): 53–63.

Towle, Jeffrey G., and Claude R. Martin, Jr. (1976). "The Elderly Consumer: One Segment or Many?" In *Advances in Consumer Research*, Vol. III, ed. Beverlee B. Anderson. Urbana, IL: Association for Consumer Research, pp. 463–468.

Yankelovich, Daniel. (1987). *The Mature Americans*. New York: Daniel Yankelovich Group, Inc.

CHAPTER 4

Older Consumer Behavior: Products

Because the mature consumer market is very heterogeneous, broad marketing strategies aimed at the entire market are likely to be ineffective. Rather, strategies must be tailored to specific market segments in order for a company to achieve efficiency in marketing efforts. The usefulness of the Life-Stage segmentation model has already been illustrated, and industry-specific segmentation has been suggested. Therefore, efforts to effectively analyze and target the mature market must focus on strategy formulation for specific life stages with regard to specific types of products and services.

The purpose of this chapter is to present the results of two large-scale national studies and analyze consumer responses to marketing offerings by segment. The results of these studies are later used (in Chapter 6) to suggest market-segment-specific strategies for selected types of products and services. Specifically, this chapter reports the consumer behavior of the four life-stage groups (healthy hermits, healthy indulgers, ailing outgoers, and frail recluses) in the following categories: food, food stores, and restaurants; apparel and footwear; pharmaceuticals; and housing. The reported results are based on responses given by older adults (age 55 and over), randomly surveyed by mail questionnaire, representing all age groups (over 55) in all 50 states. Rather than reporting percentage figures, plus (+) and minus (−) signs are used. These signs, which are reported in the tables, show deviations of the segment's behavior from the norm (average total score for the entire 55-plus market). The equals sign (=) refers to a value identical to that of the total sample. Statistically significant differences between two groups in the order of ±7 percentage points correspond to an average deviation of about 30% in relative responses given by the two groups. To the extent these deviations are significantly (statistically) different across segments, they are discussed in the text and are used as bases for strategy formulation in Chapter 6. These data should be interpreted with extreme caution. Plus and minus signs do not reflect similar levels of percentage differences across life-

Table 4.1
Past and Present Preferences for Food Products

Compared to 15-20 years ago, today	Healthy Hermits	Healthy Indulgers	Ailing Outgoers	Frail Recluses
Sacrifice good taste for good nutrition	-	-	+	+
Cookies do not taste as sweet	-	=	+	-
Same brands of frozen dinners are not as spicy	-	+	+	-
Same brands of instant coffee have more aroma	-	+	+	+
Same meals at restaurants are more spicy	-	+	-	+
More knowledgeable about nutrition	-	+	=	+

stage groups or across specific types of behaviors, and statistically significant differences between groups reflect *relative* differences.

FOOD, FOOD STORES, AND RESTAURANTS

Past and Present Preferences for Food Products

Gerontographic characteristics appear to be very strong predictors of older adults' changes in tastes and preferences over the previous 15 to 20 years. Responses to all six statements show variation across gerontographic groups (Table 4.1). While more than half of ailing outgoers now sacrifice good taste for good nutrition in comparison to their past eating habits, only four in ten of healthy hermits do the same. Ailing outgoers were also more likely to agree that the taste of cookies is not as sweet today, in comparison to frail recluses who noticed no change in the taste of cookies.

Ailing outgoers are also more likely to agree with the statement: "Same brands of frozen dinners are not as spicy," with one in three of them agreeing, in comparison to less than one in five of frail recluses. Twice as many healthy indulgers as healthy hermits agree that same brands of instant coffee have more aroma today than they did 15 to 20 years ago. Also, a greater number of healthy indulgers and frail recluses than healthy hermits think that meals at restaurants today are more spicy. Finally, healthy indulgers is the group most likely to have learned about nutrition over the previous 15 to 20 years, with nearly one in nine of them expressing knowledge gain, in comparison to healthy hermits and ailing outgoers.

Table 4.2
Reasons for Choosing Specific Brands of Foods and Alcoholic Beverages

Reasons	Healthy Hermits	Healthy Indulgers	Ailing Outgoers	Frail Recluses
Price reduction or special sale	-	+	-	+
Ease of reading information on labels or brochures	+	-	+	-
Ease of using the product	-	-	+	-
Ease of understanding and following directions provided with the product	+	-	+	-
Availability of products for people with certain physical/ health requirements	+	-	+	-
Availability of coupons	-	-	+	-
Availability of manufacturer rebates	+	-	+	-
Advice of other people your age	-	+	+	-
What others think of people who use certain brands	-	=	+	-
Their ads properly stereotype people your age	+	-	+	-
Advice/request of spouse or other relatives	-	+	-	+
Recommendation of salesperson	+	-	+	-

Reasons for Choosing Specific Brands

Gerontographic characteristics of older Americans are powerful predictors of all the factors evaluated by respondents. Based on the older person's gerontographic profile, we can predict how important each of the factors is to their brand-choice behavior concerning food products (Table 4.2). A larger percentage of healthy indulgers and frail recluses than of healthy hermits and ailing outgoers considers price reduction or special sale in their brand evaluations. Although ailing outgoers are not as sensitive to price reductions as other gerontographic groups, they are more likely to be concerned with the availability of coupons. More than three-fourths of them think availability of coupons is important, in comparison to a smaller percentage of the three remaining gerontographic groups. Also, the perceived importance of manufacturer rebates is higher among ailing outgoers and healthy hermits than among healthy indulgers.

A larger percentage of ailing outgoers than of healthy hermits, healthy indulgers, or frail recluses are concerned with ease of using food products they buy. Similarly, a higher proportion of ailing outgoers and healthy hermits, compared to a smaller percentage of healthy indulgers and frail recluses, are concerned with ease of understanding and following directions provided with the product. The former groups also show a greater propensity to consider availability of products for people with certain health requirements, again with a larger number in the first two groups expressing this orientation, compared to the responses given by healthy indulgers and frail recluses.

Ease of reading information on labels is of greater importance to ailing outgoers, in comparison to frail recluses and healthy hermits.

Healthy indulgers consider the opinion of others in their social environment while they contemplate the purchase of various food products. A larger percentage of them takes into account the advice/request of spouse or other relatives, in comparison to ailing outgoers and healthy hermits. The percentage of healthy indulgers that takes into account the advice of same-age peers is higher (along with that of ailing outgoers) than the percentage of healthy hermits and frail recluses who do the same. However, ailing outgoers is the group most sensitive to group norms, with one in four of them expressing concern about other people's evaluation of their consumer behavior. Ailing outgoers are also twice as likely as healthy indulgers and frail recluses to express concern with the way older people are portrayed in food advertisements. Finally, ailing outgoers are nearly twice as likely as frail recluses to take into account the recommendation of sales personnel in buying brands of food products and alcoholic beverages.

Store Patronage Reasons

The older person's gerontographic profile predicts the importance he or she attaches to all fourteen attributes examined (Table 4.3). Ailing outgoers perceive the majority of the factors examined to be more important than other gerontographic groups. A larger percentage of them considers ease of locating merchandise/items, in comparison to healthy indulgers and frail recluses. Nearly half of the ailing outgoers also considers the convenience of returning products or getting refunds important in their patronage decision of grocery stores, in comparison to three in ten of healthy indulgers and nearly four in ten frail recluses.

While location near one's home or place of work is an important patronage reason for food stores, it is more important to healthy indulgers and frail recluses than to healthy hermits. Ailing outgoers, and to a lesser extent healthy hermits, are more likely to patronize food stores because of their prices or special deals than other groups. The percentage of ailing outgoers who would patronize stores because they offer senior discounts is nearly double that of healthy indulgers.

A larger percentage of ailing outgoers, in comparison to frail recluses and

Table 4.3
Reasons for Patronizing Specific Food and Grocery Stores

Reasons	Healthy Hermits	Healthy Indulgers	Ailing Outgoers	Frail Recluses
Ease of locating merchandise/ items	=	-	+	=
Ease of returning products or getting refunds	+	-	+	-
Location near the place you live or work	-	+	+	+
Frequently have items on sale or special deals	+	-	+	-
Offer special discounts to customers over a certain age	+	-	+	+
Have products suitable to your physical/health needs	-	+	+	-
Have personnel who can assist you	+	-	+	-
Preference for billing/payment method	-	+	+	-
Have fast check-out registers	-	+	+	-
Offer special-assistance services (like wrapping, home delivery, package carry-out) to those who need them	+	-	+	-
Recommended by other people your age	+	-	+	-
Carry familiar brands/items	-	-	+	-
Location near several other places you patronize	-	-	+	-
Comfortable place to shop or socialize	-	-	+	-

healthy hermits, patronize stores because they have products suitable to their health needs. About half of healthy hermits and ailing outgoers considers whether the grocery store's personnel can assist them, compared to a smaller percentage of healthy indulgers and frail recluses. Twice as many ailing outgoers as frail recluses consider payment alternatives available in selecting food stores.

A larger percentage of healthy indulgers and ailing outgoers value fast check-out registers than frail recluses. Special-assistance services are of greater importance to ailing outgoers and healthy hermits, with more than four in ten reporting this reason to be a relevant patronage motive in their food-store patronage decision in comparison to nearly three in ten of healthy indulgers and frail recluses. Word-of-mouth recommendation from same-age peers is far more important to ailing outgoers than to other gerontographic groups, with frail recluses being influenced the least. A larger percentage of ailing outgoers than frail recluses values their familiarity with brands or food items, while location in relation to other stores is far more important to the former than the latter group. Finally, a higher percentage of ailing outgoers, in comparison to their healthy indulgers counterparts, indicate that they patronize food stores because they are comfortable places to shop or socialize.

Restaurant Patronage Reasons

The older person's gerontographic profile is a good predictor of the factors he or she considers most in selecting restaurants (Table 4.4). More than one in four of ailing outgoers are concerned with the ease of locating menu items, in comparison to a smaller number of healthy hermits, healthy indulgers, and frail recluses. A larger percentage of healthy indulgers and frail recluses considers location to be important in their patronage decision, in comparison to healthy hermits.

Ailing outgoers is by far the group most likely to consider senior discounts in their restaurant selection process, with nearly two-thirds of them indicating this attribute to be an important consideration. By contrast, less than half of frail recluses consider senior discounts for the same reason. About one-third of healthy indulgers, in comparison to one-fourth of healthy hermits, values assistance by personnel in choosing restaurants. Healthy indulgers is also the group most likely to be concerned with available methods for payment of meals at restaurants. Ailing outgoers and frail recluses, on the other hand, are the gerontographic groups most likely to be concerned with lines at the cash register, while ailing outgoers are twice as likely as older adults in other groups to value special-assistance services at restaurants. Half of ailing outgoers, in comparison to four in ten of healthy hermits and frail recluses, choose restaurants on the basis of same-age peer recommendation. Finally, four in ten ailing outgoers, in comparison to one in four frail recluses, consider restaurant location near other retail establishments they patronize an important factor in their restaurant patronage decision.

Payment Methods

Gerontographic profiles of older Americans are good predictors of their preferences for various payment methods. A larger percentage of healthy hermits than ailing outgoers prefers using cash to pay for their meals at restaurants. While ailing outgoers are less likely than any of the remaining gerontographic groups to prefer making use of a credit card, they are more likely than healthy hermits and healthy indulgers to write a check for the amount of their meal. Ailing outgoers are also twice as likely as healthy indulgers to use coupons with

Table 4.4
Reasons for Patronizing Specific Restaurants

Reasons	Healthy Hermits	Healthy Indulgers	Ailing Outgoers	Frail Recluses
Ease of locating merchandise/ items	-	-	+	-
Ease of returning products or getting refunds	-	-	+	+
Location near the place you live or work	-	+	+	+
Frequently have items on sale or special deals	-	=	+	-
Offer special discounts to customers over a certain age	-	-	+	-
Have products suitable to your physical/health needs	-	-	+	-
Have personnel who can assist you	-	+	+	+
Preference for billing/payment method	-	+	-	-
Have fast check-out registers	-	-	+	+
Offer special-assistance services (like wrapping, home delivery, package carry-out) to those who need them	-	-	+	-
Recommended by other people your age	-	+	+	-
Carry familiar brands/items	-	+	+	+
Location near several other places you patronize	+	-	+	-
Comfortable place to socialize	-	+	+	-

their payment, and along with frail recluses they are heavier users of senior/ member discounts than their counterparts in the two remaining gerontographic segments.

APPAREL AND FOOTWEAR

Product Ownership

Healthy indulgers and ailing outgoers are more likely than healthy hermits and frail recluses to indicate ownership of a new style of clothes or shoes.

Table 4.5
Purchase of Apparel and Footwear Products

	Healthy Hermits	Healthy Indulgers	Ailing Outgoers	Frail Recluses
Preferences for Methods of Purchasing Clothes and Shoes				
Door-to-door (at home or office)	N.A.	N.A.	N.A.	N.A.
Through the mail	+	-	-	+
By phone — you or they call	+	-	-	+
At vendor's facilities	-	+	-	+
Preferences for Sources of Information Regarding New Clothing				
Prefer to:				
See TV/print ad	+	+	-	+
Receive news in the mail	-	-	+	+
Be contacted by phone	N.A.	N.A.	N.A.	N.A.
Be visited by agent	-	+	+	+
Learn in group meetings or seminars	-	+	+	-

N.A. = Number too small to be meaningful.

Purchasing Methods

Preferences for purchasing methods differ across gerontographic groups (Table 4.5). A larger percentage of frail recluses and healthy hermits, in comparison to healthy indulgers, prefers buying through the mail. Healthy hermits are more likely than healthy indulgers to buy by phone. Finally, healthy hermits are relatively less likely than healthy indulgers and frail recluses to prefer buying apparel at stores.

Preferences for Information Sources

Gerontographic characteristics of older Americans predict their preferences for information sources regarding clothing products (Table 4.5). While two-

Table 4.6
Reasons for Choosing Specific Brands of Clothes and Shoes

Reasons	Healthy Hermits	Healthy Indulgers	Ailing Outgoers	Frail Recluses
Price reduction or special sale	-	+	+	-
Ease of reading information on labels or brochures	+	-	+	-
Ease of using the product	=	-	+	-
Ease of understanding and following directions provided with the product	+	-	+	-
Availability of products for people with certain physical/ health requirements	+	-	+	-
Availability of coupons	+	-	+	-
Availability of manufacturer rebates	+	-	+	-
Advice of other people your age	-	+	+	-
What others think of people who use certain brands	-	-	+	+
Their ads properly stereotype people your age	+	-	+	-
Advice/request of spouse or other relatives	-	+	+	+
Recommendation of salesperson	-	-	+	-

thirds of healthy indulgers prefer to see television or print ads, only half of ailing outgoers prefer the same sources. Ailing outgoers, on the other hand, are nearly twice as likely as healthy indulgers to prefer receiving information in the mail. Also, ailing outgoers are more likely than healthy hermits to prefer learning about new clothing and fashion in group meetings or seminars.

Brand Selection Criteria

The older person's reasons for choosing specific brands of clothes and shoes vary depending on his or her gerontographic characteristic (Table 4.6). A larger percentage of ailing outgoers than frail recluses considers ease of reading information on labels. Healthy hermits and ailing outgoers are twice as likely as their counterparts in the other groups to be concerned with the availability of products for people with certain physical requirements. Ailing outgoers are more likely than healthy indulgers and frail recluses to consider using coupons with their purchases. Also, a larger percentage of ailing outgoers than frail recluses would consider rebates.

Advice of same-age peers is more important to healthy indulgers and ailing outgoers than to frail recluses. Ailing outgoers are twice as likely as healthy indulgers to be concerned with what others think of people who use certain brands. Also, ailing outgoers along with healthy hermits are more concerned with proper age stereotyping in ads of apparel-brand makers, in comparison to their counterparts in the remaining two groups. Healthy indulgers rely on spouse's advice more than any other group, with healthy hermits being the gerontographic group least likely to rely on spouse. Finally, salespeople's opinion is most important to ailing outgoers and least important to healthy hermits.

Patronage Reasons

Gerontographic characteristics of older Americans are good predictors of their patronage motives (Table 4.7). Ease of locating merchandise is more important to ailing outgoers and healthy indulgers than to the other gerontographic groups. A larger percentage of ailing outgoers than healthy hermits or frail recluses considers "sales" and special deals in patronizing department stores. Senior discounts are more important to ailing outgoers and healthy hermits. There is a wide variability in preferences for billing/payment methods, with more than half of ailing outgoers considering this factor in their patronage decision, in comparison to slightly over one-third of frail recluses and healthy indulgers. Fast check-out registers are more important to ailing outgoers and healthy hermits than to healthy indulgers and frail recluses. A larger percentage of ailing outgoers and healthy indulgers, in comparison to frail recluses and healthy hermits, considers the availability of special-assistance services in patronizing department stores.

Reliance on word-of-mouth communications in choosing department stores depends on the older person's gerontographic profile as well. More than twice as many ailing outgoers as frail recluses and healthy indulgers rely on recommendation given by same-age peers. A larger percentage of ailing outgoers and healthy indulgers than healthy hermits is likely to consider brand-name familiarity of items carried by department stores. Store proximity to other places patronized is more important to ailing outgoers and healthy hermits than to the other two groups. Finally, ailing outgoers are more likely than frail recluses to consider a department store's comfort as a place to shop and socialize.

Reasons for Buying Direct

The older person's gerontographic characteristic predicts his/her likelihood of considering certain factors before buying apparel by phone or through the mail (Table 4.8). A larger percentage of frail recluses than ailing outgoers considers price. Ailing outgoers, however, are more likely than frail recluses and healthy hermits to consider the availability of free pick-up service for returns. A larger

Table 4.7
Reasons for Patronizing Department Stores

Reasons	Healthy Hermits	Healthy Indulgers	Ailing Outgoers	Frail Recluses
Ease of locating merchandise/items	-	+	+	-
Ease of returning products or getting refunds	-	+	+	-
Location near the place you live or work	=	-	-	+
Frequently have items on sale or special deals	-	+	+	-
Offer special discounts to customers over a certain age	+	-	+	-
Have products suitable to your physical/health needs	-	-	+	-
Have personnel who can assist you	+	+	-	-
Preference for billing/payment method	-	-	+	-
Have fast check-out registers	+	-	+	-
Offer special-assistance services (like wrapping, home delivery, package carry-out) to those who need them	-	+	+	-
Recommended by other people your age	+	-	+	-
Carry familiar brands/items	-	+	+	-
Location near several other places you patronize	+	-	+	-
Comfortable place to shop or socialize	-	-	+	-

percentage of healthy indulgers than ailing outgoers is likely to consider product selection. Finally, both ailing outgoers and healthy hermits are more likely than healthy indulgers to consider days one must wait before receiving apparel ordered direct.

PHARMACEUTICAL PRODUCTS

Product Use

The older person's gerontographic profile predicts usage of prescription drugs (Table 4.9). Ailing outgoers are more likely than healthy hermits and healthy

Table 4.8
Reasons Considered Before Buying Clothes and Shoes by Phone or Through the Mail

Reasons Considered	Healthy Hermits	Healthy Indulgers	Ailing Outgoers	Frail Recluses
Price (including shipping (charges)	=	-	-	+
Type of credit card accepted	-	+	+	-
Return/cancellation and refund policy	-	+	-	+
Convenience, in comparison to other ways of buying the same product/service	+	=	=	-
Free pick-up service for returns	-	+	+	-
Availability of toll free (800) number	+	-	+	-
Selection of products or services	-	+	-	+
Days to wait before receiving	+	-	+	-

indulgers to use one or more prescription drugs. Also, the older person's gerontographic characteristic can predict his or her likelihood of using hair-care and face-care products. Ailing outgoers and healthy indulgers use the most; frail recluses use the least; while healthy hermits also show a relatively low usage.

Preference for Information Sources

The older person's gerontographic profile is a fairly good predictor of his or her preference for certain types of information sources regarding new drug and cosmetic products (Table 4.9). A larger percentage of healthy indulgers and frail recluses than ailing outgoers prefers receiving information via television and print ads. However, more than one-third of ailing outgoers prefers receiving news in the mail, in comparison to their counterparts in other gerontographic segments. A relatively larger percent of ailing outgoers than healthy hermits prefers to hear about new products from sales representatives who would visit them; and more than twice as many ailing outgoers as frail recluses prefer hearing the news in group meetings or seminars.

Brand Selection Criteria

Older persons differ most on the basis of their gerontographic profile when it comes to choosing brands of drugs and health aids (Table 4.10). The importance of each one of the specific factors differs on the basis of the older person's

Table 4.9
Purchase and Consumption of Pharmaceutical Products

Products Used	Healthy Hermits	Healthy Indulgers	Ailing Outgoers	Frail Recluses
Prescription drug for chronic condition	-	-	+	-
Hair-care or face-care products	-	+	+	-
Preferences for Sources of Information Regarding New Drugs and Cosmetics				
See TV/print ad	+	+	-	+
Receive news in the mail	-	-	+	+
Be contacted by phone	-	+	+	-
Be visited by agent	-	+	+	+
Learn in group meetings or seminars	+	+	+	-

gerontographic profile. Price reduction or special sales is more important to healthy hermits and ailing outgoers than to healthy indulgers and frail recluses. Also, a larger percentage of healthy hermits and ailing outgoers than healthy indulgers reports that ease of reading information on labels and brochures is important in their brand decisions concerning drugs and health aids. Ease of using drugs and health aids is more important to ailing outgoers and least important to frail recluses. Ease of understanding and following directions provided with the product is also more important to ailing outgoers and healthy hermits than to the remaining gerontographic groups.

Availability of products for people with certain health/physical requirements is most important to ailing outgoers and least important to frail recluses. Nearly twice as many ailing outgoers as frail recluses are concerned with coupons in choosing specific brands of drugs and health aids. The same appears to be true for manufacturer rebates. Advice of same-age peers is much more important to ailing outgoers than to the remaining gerontographic groups, with nearly half of them admitting to social influence, in comparison to roughly one-third of the older adults in the remaining gerontographic groups. Also, with respect to social influence, what others think of the older person's brand choice is more important to ailing outgoers and least important to healthy indulgers. Age stereotyping in ads is also of greatest concern to ailing outgoers and of least concern to healthy indulgers. While about one in three of healthy hermits and frail recluses responds to advice/request of spouse or other relatives, four in ten of the ailing outgoers do the same. Finally, the recommendation of a salesperson is more important to

Table 4.10
Reasons for Choosing Specific Brands of Drugs and Health Aids

Reasons	Healthy Hermits	Healthy Indulgers	Ailing Outgoers	Frail Recluses
Price reduction or special sale	+	-	+	-
Ease of reading information on labels or brochures	+	-	+	-
Ease of using the product	-	-	+	-
Ease of understanding and following directions provided with the product	+	-	+	-
Availability of products for people with certain physical/health requirements	-	-	+	-
Availability of coupons	+	-	+	-
Availability of manufacturer rebates	+	-	+	-
Advice of other people your age	-	-	+	-
What others think of people who use certain brands	-	-	+	-
Their ads properly stereotype people your age	-	-	+	-
Advice/request of spouse or other relatives	-	+	+	-
Recommendation of salesperson	+	-	+	-

ailing outgoers, with one in four of them admitting to this influence, in comparison to one in seven of the healthy indulgers.

Patronage Reasons

Gerontographic characteristics are very strong predictors of the older person's perceptions of the importance of nearly all fourteen patronage factors examined (Table 4.11). Fewer of the frail recluses think that ease of locating merchandise is important, in comparison to their older counterparts in the remaining gerontographic groups who are of the same opinion. Ease of returning products or getting refunds is important to a larger percentage of ailing outgoers than healthy indulgers or healthy hermits. Healthy hermits is the group least likely to be concerned about location of drug stores or pharmacies.

Special deals or sales tend to be of greater appeal to ailing outgoers and healthy hermits. Senior discounts are by far a more important patronage motive for ailing outgoers than older adults in the remaining gerontographic groups. More ailing outgoers mentioned this reason to be important in their drug store

Table 4.11
Reasons for Patronizing Specific Drug Stores/Pharmacies

Reasons	Healthy Hermits	Healthy Indulgers	Ailing Outgoers	Frail Recluses
Ease of locating merchandise/items	+	+	+	-
Ease of returning products or getting refunds	-	-	+	-
Location near the place you live or work	-	+	+	+
Frequently have items on sale or special deals	+	-	+	-
Offer special discounts to customers over a certain age	-	-	+	-
Have products suitable to your physical/ health needs	-	-	+	-
Have personnel who can assist you	=	-	+	-
Preference for billing/payment method	-	+	+	-
Have fast check-out registers	-	+	+	-
Offer special-assistance services (like wrapping, home delivery, package carry-out) to those who need them	-	-	+	-
Recommended by other people your age	+	-	+	-
Carry familiar brands/items	-	-	+	-
Location near several other places you patronize	+	-	+	-
Comfortable place to shop or socialize	+	-	+	+

or pharmacy patronage decision, in comparison to older people in other groups. Ailing outgoers are also more concerned with product suitability to their physical/health needs than other gerontographic groups; frail recluses are the least demanding. Personnel assistance is also more important to ailing outgoers than to healthy indulgers or frail recluses.

Three other patronage factors are more important to ailing outgoers than frail recluses: preference for billing/payment methods, fast check-out, and location near several other places patronized. Special-assistance services are important to one in four ailing outgoers, in comparison to one in ten frail recluses and healthy indulgers, and to one in six of healthy hermits. Personal recommendation of same-age peers is at least three times more important to ailing outgoers than to older adults in other gerontographic groups. Similarly, availability of familiar brands is a more important factor to ailing outgoers, with nearly two-thirds of them indicating importance, compared to just over half of older adults in the

Table 4.12
Purchase of Pharmaceutical Products

Preferences for Methods of Purchasing Prescription Drugs	Healthy Hermits	Healthy Indulgers	Ailing Outgoers	Frail Recluses
Door-to-door (at home or office)	N.A.	N.A.	N.A.	N.A.
Through the mail	-	-	+	+
By phone — you or they call	+	-	+	+
At vendor's facilities	=	-	=	+
Preferences for Methods of Purchasing Cosmetics and Health Aids				
Door-to-door (at home or office)	-	+	+	-
Through the mail	-	-	+	+
By phone — you or they call	+	-	-	-
At vendor's facilities	-	+	-	+

N.A. = Number too small to be meaningful.

three remaining groups. Finally, healthy hermits, ailing outgoers, and frail recluses are more likely to consider drug stores and pharmacies as places for socializing, with at least three in ten of older adults in these groups indicating importance, in comparison to nearly one in five healthy indulgers.

Purchasing Methods

The older person's gerontographic profile is a fairly good predictor of his or her preference for the various methods of purchasing prescription drugs (Table 4.12). Although only a small percentage of older adults would buy from door-to-door salespeople, those most likely to buy are the healthy indulgers. Ailing outgoers are more likely than healthy hermits to buy through the mail. Finally, frail recluses are more likely to prefer retail establishments as sources of prescription drugs.

Gerontographics also predict preferences for three of the four methods of distribution of cosmetics and health-aids (Table 4.12). Ailing outgoers and frail recluses are more likely than healthy indulgers to prefer buying these products through the mail. Older adults who buy by phone are more likely to be healthy hermits than frail recluses. A larger percentage of frail recluses and healthy indulgers than healthy hermits or ailing outgoers prefers purchasing cosmetics and health-aids at retail establishments.

Table 4.13
Direct Buying and Payment for Pharmaceutical Products

Reasons Considered Before Buying Health Aid and Drugs by Phone or Mail	Healthy Hermits	Healthy Indulgers	Ailing Outgoers	Frail Recluses
Price (including shipping charges)	-	+	+	-
Type of credit card accepted	-	-	+	-
Return/cancellation and refund policy	-	-	+	-
Convenience, in comparison to other ways of buying the same product/service	=	-	+	-
Free pick-up service for returns	-	-	+	-
Availability of toll free (800) number	-	-	+	-
Selection of products or services	-	+	+	-
Days to wait before receiving	-	+	+	-
Preferences for Payment Methods for Prescription Drugs				
Cash	+	+	-	-
Check	-	-	+	+
Credit card	+	-	-	+
Coupon	+	-	+	-
Senior/member discount	-	-	+	+

Reasons for Buying Direct

The importance of each of the eight reasons examined before buying direct depends on the older person's gerontographic profile, with ailing outgoers being the group most likely to consider the largest number of factors (Table 4.13). A larger percentage of ailing outgoers than of healthy hermits and frail recluses would consider price. Type of credit card accepted is more important to ailing outgoers than to older adults in the remaining gerontographic groups. Also, a larger percentage of ailing outgoers than healthy indulgers considers the seller's cancellation/return and refund policy.

A larger percentage of ailing outgoers than frail recluses and healthy indulgers mentions convenience in buying direct. Ailing outgoers are also more likely than older adults in the remaining gerontographic groups to consider availability of toll-free (800) number and product selection. Finally, days to wait before receiving the product ordered is more important to ailing outgoers than to healthy hermits and frail recluses.

Payment Methods

The older person's gerontographic characteristic predicts rather well preference for payment methods concerning prescription drugs (Table 4.13). Healthy hermits are more likely to prefer cash than ailing outgoers. Ailing outgoers are more likely than healthy indulgers to prefer paying by check. A larger percentage of frail recluses than ailing outgoers and healthy indulgers prefers paying by credit card. While use of coupons is very low, ailing outgoers prefer using coupons more than healthy indulgers. Finally, senior/member discounts are more likely to be preferred by frail recluses and ailing outgoers, with about half of them expressing preference, in comparison to less than half of healthy indulgers and healthy hermits.

HOUSING PREFERENCES

Preferences for various types of housing vary by gerontographic characteristics of older Americans, whether such preferences are examined in terms of present type of housing or future type of housing arrangements preferred (Table 4.14). While gerontographic characteristics do not strongly predict preference for single-family houses, healthy indulgers are more likely than healthy hermits and frail recluses to live in apartments, townhouses, or condominiums. A larger percentage of ailing outgoers than frail recluses lives in retirement communities with health-care services. Gerontographic differences in preferences for future housing plans also exist. Interestingly, nearly twice as many frail recluses as ailing outgoers prefer to live in a single-family home. More ailing outgoers than healthy hermits plan to move into a retirement community with health-care services. Nearly twice as many healthy indulgers and ailing outgoers as healthy hermits and frail recluses plan to move into a nursing home.

Reasons for Moving

Gerontographic characteristics are rather good predictors of the older person's perceptions of the reasons one moves into various types of housing facilities (Table 4.14). The older person's gerontographic characteristics are strong predictors of the types of reasons one gives for moving into an *apartment, townhouse, or condominium*. More healthy indulgers than older adults in other gerontographic groups indicate loss of spouse as the main reason for moving. A much larger percentage of frail recluses than older adults in other gerontographic groups thinks that unwillingness or inability to do house chores is a reason for moving. A larger percentage of healthy indulgers than healthy hermits and ailing outgoers thinks that people move into these types of housing facilities

Table 4.14
Housing Preferences

Present Type of Housing	Healthy Hermits	Healthy Indulgers	Ailing Outgoers	Frail Recluses
Single family house	=	-	-	+
Apartment/townhouse/condominium	-	+	+	-
Retirement community without health-care services	+	-	+	-
Retirement community with health-care services	-	+	+	-
Nursing home	N.A.	N.A.	N.A.	N.A.
Plans for Future Type of Housing				
Single family house	-	+	-	+
Apartment/townhouse condominium	-	+	+	-
Retirement community without health-care services	-	+	-	+
Retirement community with health-care services	-	-	+	+
Nursing home	-	+	+	-

N.A. = Number too small to be meaningful.

to reduce housing costs. However, the proportion of older adults in the four gerontographic groups who says people move into these facilities in order to be closer to relatives is the lowest for healthy indulgers than for any of the remaining three groups.

Ailing outgoers are more likely than healthy indulgers and frail recluses to mention that need for continuous health-care assistance as well as access to personal-care services are reasons for moving into an apartment, townhouse, or condominium. Finally, frail recluses are more likely to indicate that freedom and independence are important reasons why people move into an apartment, townhouse, or condominium, in comparison to ailing outgoers, healthy hermits, and healthy indulgers.

Gerontographic characteristics are strong predictors of the older person's propensity to give various reasons for moving into a *retirement community* (table 4.15). While older adults feel that loss of spouse is an important reason why older people move into a retirement community, regardless of gerontographic profile, they differ a great deal in their responses based on their gerontographic

Table 4.15
Reasons for Moving into Various Types of Housing Facilities

Reasons for Moving Into an Apartment, Townhouse or Condominium	Healthy Hermits	Healthy Indulgers	Ailing Outgoers	Frail Recluses
Loss of spouse	-	+	-	+
Unwilling or unable to do house chores	-	+	-	+
To reduce housing costs	-	+	-	+
To be closer to relatives	+	-	+	+
Need for continuous health-care assistance	=	-	+	-
To have access to personal-care services	-	-	+	-
To have more social contacts and activities	=	-	+	-
To have freedom and independence	-	+	-	+
Reasons for Moving Into a Retirement Community				
Loss of spouse	=	-	+	-
Unwilling or unable to do house chores	-	+	-	+
To reduce housing costs	+	-	+	-
To be closer to relatives	-	-	+	-
Need for continuous health-care assistance	-	+	+	-
To have access to personal-care services	-	+	+	-
To have more social contacts and activities	-	+	=	-
To have freedom and independence	=	+	+	-
Loss of spouse	-	+	-	+
Unwilling or unable to do house chores	+	+	-	+
To reduce housing costs	+	+	-	+
To be closer to relatives	=	-	+	+
Need for continuous health-care assistance	-	+	-	+

Table 4.15 (Continued)

Reasons for Moving Into a Nursing Home	Healthy Hermits	Healthy Indulgers	Ailing Outgoers	Frail Recluses
To have access to personal-care services	-	+	-	+
To have more social contacts and activities	-	+	+	-
To have freedom and independence	+	+	=	-

characteristics. Unwillingness or inability to do house chores is a reason most likely to be given by frail recluses; it is more likely to be cited by this group than by ailing outgoers or healthy hermits. Lower housing costs is an important reason for moving into this type of housing among ailing outgoers, much more so than among healthy indulgers. Frail recluses are also less likely than ailing outgoers to mention this reason. Ailing outgoers are also more likely than older adults in other groups to say that being close to relatives is a reason for moving into a retirement community. Need for continuous health-care assistance is given as a reason for moving by a larger percentage of healthy indulgers and ailing outgoers than by frail recluses and healthy hermits. A larger percentage of healthy indulgers than healthy hermits and frail recluses reports access to personal-care services as a reason for moving into a retirement community. Also, a larger percentage of healthy indulgers than frail recluses indicates social contacts and activities as reasons for moving. Finally, frail recluses are least likely to mention freedom and independence as a reason for moving into a retirement community.

Gerontographic characteristics predict responses to three reasons for moving into a *nursing home* (Table 4.15). A larger percentage of frail recluses than healthy hermits and ailing outgoers indicates loss of spouse to be a reason for moving into a nursing home. More healthy indulgers and frail recluses than older adults in other groups think that older people move into a nursing home because they need continuous health-care assistance. More frail recluses are of the opinion that people move out of a single-family house into a nursing home in order to have access to personal-care services, in comparison to ailing outgoers and healthy hermits.

Reasons for Choosing Specific Homes

Perceptions of motives for choosing specific homes differ across gerontographic groups (Table 4.16). Older adults differ with regard to the reasons they cite for choosing a *single-family house* based on their gerontographic profiles. Location is more important to healthy hermits and ailing outgoers, with six in

Table 4.16
Reasons for Choosing a Specific Home

Single Family House	Healthy Hermits	Healthy Indulgers	Ailing Outgoers	Frail Recluses
Location near shopping centers	+	-	+	-
Distance from friends and relatives	+	-	+	-
Access to medical services	-	-	+	+
Access to personal and home-care services	+	-	+	+
Access to planned social activities	+	-	+	-
Home or personal security	-	-	+	+
Location near hospitals	+	-	+	+
Access to public transportation	+	-	+	-
Advice of relatives	+	-	+	-
Apartment, Townhouse or Condominium				
Location near shopping centers	-	+	+	+
Distance from friends and relatives	-	+	+	+
Access to medical services	-	+	+	+
Access to personal and home-care services	-	+	+	+
Access to planned social activities	-	-	+	-
Home or personal security	-	+	-	+
Location near hospitals	-	-	+	+
Access to public transportation	-	+	+	-
Advice of relatives	-	+	+	-

ten of people in these groups citing this reason, in comparison to a little over half of healthy indulgers. These groups also differ with respect to the emphasis they place on the distance of the house from friends and relatives, with the former groups placing more emphasis on this factor than the latter group. Access to medical services is of greater concern to ailing outgoers and frail recluses than to healthy indulgers. The latter group is also the least concerned with accessibility to personal and home-care services.

Access to planned social activities is valued nearly twice as much by ailing outgoers than by healthy indulgers and frail recluses. Location near hospitals is a less significant factor among healthy indulgers than among other geronto-graphic groups. Access to public transportation is valued by a larger percentage of ailing outgoers and healthy hermits than by healthy indulgers and frail re-cluses. Twice as many ailing outgoers and healthy hermits as frail recluses are likely to consider advice from relatives in choosing a single-family house, al-though this factor is not considered to be important in this type of housing selection.

Gerontographic characteristics are very strong predictors of the older person's propensity to consider various reasons in choosing an *apartment, townhouse, or condominium* (Table 4.16). More than half of the healthy indulgers, in compar-ison to four in ten of healthy hermits, consider location near shopping centers important in choosing such housing facilities. While one-fourth of healthy her-mits consider distance from friends and relatives to be important, the percentage for older adults in the remaining groups that does the same is over one-third. Approximately four in ten ailing outgoers and frail recluses consider proximity to medical services to be an important reason people choose an apartment, town-house, or condominium, but a relatively smaller percentage of healthy hermits is of the same opinion.

Access to personal and home-care services is valued by one-third of healthy indulgers and by three in ten ailing outgoers and frail recluses; yet less than one-fourth of healthy hermits feels the same way. However, access to planned personal activities is more important to ailing outgoers than to frail recluses in choosing these types of homes. The differences in perceptions of the importance of home or personal security are even more striking among the four groups. While slightly more than half of the healthy indulgers and frail recluses consider this factor to be important, a smaller percentage of healthy hermits and ailing outgoers considers it to be important in choosing an apartment, condominium, or townhouse. Location near hospitals is an attribute considered most important by ailing outgoers, in comparison to healthy hermits and healthy indulgers. Ac-cess to public transportation is of greater importance to ailing outgoers than to healthy hermits and frail recluses. Finally, ailing outgoers are twice as likely as frail recluses to consider the opinion of relatives in choosing these types of housing facilities. Responses to this factor by older adults in the two remaining gerontographic groups are also lower than those of ailing outgoers.

Gerontographics are powerful predictors of older adults' perceptions of the importance of various factors in choosing a *retirement community* (Table 4.16). Healthy indulgers and frail recluses are those most likely to indicate that location near shopping centers is an important consideration, while healthy hermits is the group least concerned with this factor. Distance from friends and relatives shows the same pattern among the four groups, and so does access to medical services. Access to personal and home-care services is least important among healthy hermits; it is of nearly equal importance among the remaining gerontographic groups. Healthy indulgers are more likely than healthy hermits to value access to planned social activities. Home or personal security is of least importance to healthy hermits, and so is access to public transportation. Finally, ailing outgoers are more likely than healthy hermits and frail recluses to perceive the advice of relatives as an important factor in selecting a retirement community.

Reasons for choosing a *nursing home* are significantly related to the older person's gerontographic background (Table 4.16). Frail recluses are nearly twice as likely as healthy hermits to cite location near shopping centers as an important reason for choosing this type of housing facility. Healthy indulgers and frail recluses are more likely than healthy hermits and ailing outgoers to indicate distance from friends and relatives, access to medical services, and location near hospitals as important reasons for choosing a nursing home. A larger percentage of healthy indulgers than older adults in any of the remaining gerontographic groups is likely to mention access to planned social services, with about one-fourth of them expressing this view.

Preferences for Sources of Information

Gerontographic characteristics of older Americans are the best predictors of the sources of information preferred. Half of healthy hermits prefer to find out about new housing options from television or print ads, but fewer ailing outgoers and frail recluses prefer ads. Healthy hermits are the group least likely to prefer receiving news in the mail, with slightly more than one-fifth of older adults in this group expressing preference for this source, compared with over one-third of ailing outgoers and about three in ten of the older adults in the remaining gerontographic groups. A larger percentage of healthy indulgers and frail recluses than healthy hermits and ailing outgoers prefers to be visited by an agent. Finally, learning in group meetings or seminars is preferred by a larger percentage of healthy indulgers and ailing outgoers than by healthy hermits and frail recluses.

CHAPTER 5

Older Consumer Behavior: Services

In line with the rationale given in the previous chapter, the present chapter is a continuation of the presentation of the results of the two large-scale national studies. Specifically, this chapter reports the consumer behavior of the four life-stage segments in the following types of service categories: mass media, travel and leisure, financial services, high-tech, health care, and insurance. The reported results are based on responses given by older Americans (age 55 and over), who were randomly surveyed by mail questionnaire, representing all age groups of the 55-plus population in all 50 states. Again, rather than reporting percentages, plus (+) and minus (−) signs are used in the tables to show whether the segment's behavior is above or below the norm for the entire (over 55) market. The equals sign (=) suggests the segment's behavior is equal to the norm. Only statistically significant deviations are discussed in the text and are used in the next chapter as bases for strategy formulation.

MASS MEDIA USE

Significant variations exist across the four gerontographic groups when it comes to the media-use habits of these segments (Table 5.1). Ailing outgoers and frail recluses watch premium television cable the most. Healthy hermits read the newspaper and listen to the radio less than those in the other three groups; and they make the least use of VCRs. Ailing outgoers are the heaviest viewers of television, while healthy indulgers and frail recluses are the lightest viewers of this medium.

The groups' magazine readership habits were also examined by asking respondents to write the names of the magazines they read on a regular basis. Due to the large number of magazines that respondents mentioned, we have grouped most of the magazines into broad categories based on the dominant themes or contents of these magazines. Table 5.2 shows types of magazines read by geron-

Table 5.1
Consumption of Mass Media–Related Products and Services

Media Use	Healthy Hermits	Healthy Indulgers	Ailing Outgoers	Frail Recluses
Watch premium TV cable channels (once or more a week)	-	-	+	+
Read the newspaper (every day)	-	+	+	+
Listen to the radio (every day)	-	+	+	+
Watch comedy and variety TV shows (several times a week)	-	-	+	-
Watch adventure and drama TV shows (several times a week)	+	-	+	-
Watch TV news and documentaries (every day)	+	-	+	-
Use VCR to record or play movies (once or more a week)	-	+	+	+
Preferences for Methods of Purchasing Books, Magazines, and Videocassettes				
Door-to-door (at home or office)	+	+	-	+
Through the mail	-	-	+	+
By phone — you or they call	+	-	+	+
At vendor's facilities	+	-	-	+

tographic groups. Gerontographic characteristics of older Americans were found to be the strongest predictors of their magazine readership habits, predicting readership for nearly all of the general types of magazines identified. The following types of magazines show only the gerontographic group that can be identified as having the highest readership. (The group's readership level may differ substantially or very little from other groups; and readership across different types of heavily read magazines across the same group varies as well.)

Magazines for the aged	Ailing outgoers
"Health/nutrition" magazines	Ailing outgoers
"Food/cooking" magazines	Frail recluses
"Travel/leisure/geography/history" magazines	Frail recluses
"Business (professional)" magazines	Healthy indulgers
"Homes/decorating" magazines	Frail recluses
"News & public affairs" magazines	Healthy indulgers

Table 5.2
Magazine Readership

Type of Magazines	Healthy Hermits	Healthy Indulgers	Ailing Outgoers	Frail Recluses
Magazines for the "aged"	-	-	+	+
Health/nutrition	-	-	+	-
Food/cooking	-	+	+	+
Travel/leisure, geography and history	-	+	-	+
Business (professional)	-	+	-	+
Homes/decorating	-	-	+	+
Consumer finances/money	-	+	+	+
News and public affairs	-	+	-	+
Sports/athletics (spectator)	-	+	-	-
Sports/athletics/fitness (participant)	-	+	-	+
Family	+	-	+	-
Wildlife/nature/outdoors	-	+	=	+
Games/entertainment/hobbies	+	+	-	+
Arts & sciences	-	+	-	+
"Do-it-yourself"	-	-	-	+
General interest – women	-	-	+	-
General interest – all	-	-	+	-
Religion	+	+	=	-

"Sports (spectator)" magazines	Healthy indulgers
"Sports (participant)" magazines	Healthy indulgers
"General interest (women)" magazines	Ailing outgoers
"General interest (all)" magazines	Ailing outgoers
"Religion" magazines	Healthy indulgers

Finally, there are differences in preferences for purchasing methods regarding mass-media products based on the older person's gerontographic characteristic (Table 5.1). A larger percentage of frail recluses than healthy hermits prefers to buy magazines, books, and videocassettes through the mail. Also, a larger percentage of frail recluses, ailing outgoers, and healthy hermits, in comparison to healthy indulgers, prefer to buy these products by phone. Finally, buying at stores is a more preferred purchasing method among frail recluses than among ailing outgoers and healthy indulgers.

TRAVEL AND LEISURE SERVICES

Preferences for Travel and Leisure Services

Older Americans with different gerontographic profiles are likely to show different preferences for the four travel- and leisure-related services examined (Table 5.3). Specifically, more healthy indulgers and ailing outgoers than healthy hermits and frail recluses either use or would like to use airline package deals. Ailing outgoers are twice as likely to prefer travel clubs or programs than healthy hermits. Healthy indulgers is the group most likely to show interest in foreign travel, having or expressing desire for having a valid passport, in comparison to frail recluses and ailing outgoers. Finally, ailing outgoers are more likely than healthy hermits and frail recluses to express preference for restaurant clubs.

Preferences for Sources of Information

The older person's gerontographic characteristic predicts preference for television or print ads, with the healthy hermits being the group most likely to show preference and the ailing outgoers the group least likely to prefer information from ads in these media regarding travel packages (Table 5.3). However, healthy hermits are least likely to prefer learning about such services in group meetings or seminars, in comparison to ailing outgoers, which is the group most likely to prefer this information source.

Purchasing Methods

The older person's gerontographic profile predicts fairly well his or her preference for three of the four methods examined: door-to-door, mail, and at the vendor's facilities (Table 5.3). Healthy indulgers and ailing outgoers are more likely than frail recluses to prefer door-to-door purchase of vacation packages. Ailing outgoers are more likely than healthy hermits and healthy indulgers to prefer buying vacation packages through the mail. Finally, ailing outgoers are more likely than frail recluses to prefer purchasing travel-related services at vendor's facilities.

Reasons for Patronizing Airlines/Cruise Lines

Gerontographic characteristics of older Americans are strong predictors of their perceptions of the importance of most of the patronage factors examined concerning the choice of airlines and cruise lines (Table 5.4). Prices are of

Table 5.3
Preferences for Travel and Leisure Services, Sources of Information, and
Purchasing Methods

Services	Healthy Hermits	Healthy Indulgers	Ailing Outgoers	Frail Recluses
Airline Package (fly anywhere for the same price)	-	+	+	-
Travel club or program where you pay $50-$100 to join and you get discounted rates and rebates	-	+	+	=
Valid passport	=	+	-	-
Restaurant club where you pay about $30 to join and get discounts at member restaurants	-	+	+	-
Preferences for Sources of Information Regarding New Vacation/Travel Packages				
Prefer to:				
See TV/print ad	+	+	-	+
Receive news in the mail	-	-	+	+
Be contacted by phone	-	+	-	+
Be visited by agent	-	+	-	+
Learn in group meetings or seminars	-	+	+	+
Methods of Purchasing Vacation Packages				
Door-to-door (at home or office)	-	+	+	-
Through the mail	-	-	+	+
By phone — you or they call	-	+	-	+
At vendor's facilities	+	-	+	-

greater concern to healthy indulgers than to ailing outgoers and healthy hermits. Nearly six out of ten of the former group, compared to less than half of the other two groups, are concerned with prices. However, about half of the healthy indulgers and ailing outgoers, in comparison to a smaller percentage of healthy hermits and frail recluses, indicate discounts to age groups (seniors) as a reason for patronage. Also, special deals through membership programs are of greater interest to the healthy indulgers than to older adults in other gerontographic groups.

Table 5.4
Reasons for Patronizing Airlines/Cruise Lines

Reasons for Patronizing	Healthy Hermits	Healthy Indulgers	Ailing Outgoers	Frail Recluses
Reasonable prices or fees	-	+	-	+
Convenience in reaching the service provider	-	+	-	+
Ease of getting related services at the same place	-	+	+	-
Explanation of various services by staff/personnel	-	+	+	-
Personnel/staff assistance with filling out forms	-	+	-	=
Discounts to age groups (children, seniors)	-	+	+	-
Preference for billing/payment methods	-	+	+	-
You like the way their ads show people your age	-	+	+	-
Special deals through group or membership programs	-	+	-	+
Advice of children or close relatives	-	+	+	-
Advice of other people your age	-	+	+	-
Referrals/endorsements by firms or professionals	+	+	-	-
Ease of doing business by phone or by mail	+	+	+	-

Age stereotypes in advertisements are more popular among ailing outgoers than other gerontographic groups. A smaller percentage of healthy indulgers expresses a similar view. Healthy hermits and frail recluses are the least concerned about age stereotypes in ads. Slightly more than one in five of frail recluses considers the ease of doing business by phone or by mail, in comparison to approximately three in ten of older adults in the remaining gerontographic groups. Ease of getting related services at the same place is more important to healthy indulgers than to healthy hermits. Also, healthy indulgers are more likely than frail recluses to request explanation of various services from staff/personnel when choosing airlines or cruise lines. A larger percentage of healthy indulgers than of other gerontographic groups also values personnel/staff assistance with filling out forms. The same group is more concerned than ailing outgoers with

Table 5.5
Reasons for Patronizing Hotels/Motels

Reasons for Patronizing	Healthy Hermits	Healthy Indulgers	Ailing Outgoers	Frail Recluses
Reasonable prices or fees	+	+	-	+
Convenience in reaching the service provider	+	+	-	+
Ease of getting related services at the same place	+	-	+	-
Explanation of various services by staff/personnel	-	+	-	+
Personnel/staff assistance with filling out forms	-	+	+	-
Discounts to age groups (children, seniors)	-	-	+	+
Preference for billing/payment methods	-	+	-	-
You like the way their ads show people your age	-	-	+	+
Special deals through group or membership programs	-	+	+	+
Advice of children or close relatives	+	=	-	-
Advice of other people your age	+	+	-	-
Referrals/endorsements by firms or professionals	+	+	-	-
Ease of doing business by phone or by mail	-	+	-	+

the billing or payment methods available to them and with the advice they receive from other people of their age. Finally, healthy hermits tend to rely more on referrals than frail recluses in their patronage decision concerning airlines and cruise lines.

Reasons for Patronizing Hotels/Motels

The perceived importance of hotel/motel patronage factors is not uniform across older adults possessing different gerontographic profiles (Table 5.5). Ailing outgoers are least concerned with prices and convenience in reaching the particular hotel/motel, but are most concerned with the proper age stereotypes in advertisements than other gerontographic groups. Senior discounts are of

Table 5.6
Preferences for Methods of Payment for Airline Tickets, Hotel/Motel Accommodations, and Meals at Restaurants

Airline Tickets	Healthy Hermits	Healthy Indulgers	Ailing Outgoers	Frail Recluses
Cash	+	+	-	-
Check	-	-	+	+
Credit Card	+	+	-	+
Coupon	-	-	+	+
Senior/member discount	-	+	+	+
Hotel/Motel Accommodations				
Cash	+	-	-	=
Check	-	-	+	+
Credit Card	+	+	-	+
Coupon	-	-	+	+
Senior/member discount	-	+	=	+

greatest importance to frail recluses, with nearly seven in ten of them expressing interest. Healthy hermits and healthy indulgers are the groups least likely to be concerned with senior discounts. Special deals through group or membership programs are of least interest to healthy hermits than to any of the remaining gerontographic groups. Finally, healthy indulgers and ailing outgoers are more likely than healthy hermits to consider hotel/motel personnel's assistance in filling out forms.

Payment Methods

While cash as a form of payment for airline tickets shows little variation across gerontographic segments, use of checks and credit varies across the four groups (Table 5.6). A check is the preferred method of payment among frail recluses. Use of a check is lowest among healthy indulgers, with the older adults in this group expressing preference for payment of airline tickets by check. On the other hand, healthy indulgers prefer using credit to pay for this transportation service, more so than ailing outgoers. While only half of the healthy hermits prefer using senior/member discounts, about six in ten older adults in the remaining gerontographic groups prefer to use this option.

The older person's gerontographic profile is a good predictor of most of his or her preferences for methods of payment for lodging services (Table 5.6).

Table 5.7
Preferences for Financial Services and Use of Credit Cards

Preferences for Financial Services	Healthy Hermits	Healthy Indulgers	Ailing Outgoers	Frail Recluses
Professional financial advice on investments for a fee	-	+	+	-
Automatic deposit of your check (EFT)	+	+	+	-
Overdraft privilege or personal line of credit	-	+	-	+
Free financial services for keeping large balances	-	+	-	-
Risky investments that could produce much higher than average income	-	+	+	-
Average-risk investments producing an average level of income	-	+	-	-
Safe investments that could produce lower than average income	-	+	-	-
Use of Credit Cards				
Used in past 6 months				
Visa	-	+	+	-
Discover	-	+	-	+
MasterCard	+	+	-	-
American Express	+	+	-	-
Department store card	-	+	-	+
Diners Club or Carte Blanche	-	+	+	-
Gasoline card	-	+	-	+
Number of credit cards used				
0	+	-	+	-
1-3	+	-	+	-
4 or more	-	+	-	+

Preferences for cash and coupons as methods of payment show no variation across gerontographic segments. Check is the most preferred method of payment among ailing outgoers; it is the least preferred by healthy indulgers. The latter group shows the highest preference for credit as a method of payment for lodging services. Senior/member discounts are preferred mostly by frail recluses.

FINANCIAL SERVICES

Preferences for Financial Services

Gerontographic characteristics are good predictors of the older person's preferences for professional financial services (Table 5.7). Healthy indulgers are more likely than any of the remaining groups to express preferences for receiving *financial advice*. Older adults in this group are more likely than frail recluses and healthy hermits to express preference for professional financial advice on investments for a fee. Ailing outgoers are the second group most likely to express such preferences. Differences in preferences for *overdraft privilege* or *personal line of credit* were found among gerontographic groups. Healthy hermits prefer this service the least, while healthy indulgers and frail recluses prefer it the most. Healthy indulgers also prefer *free financial services* for keeping large balances more than healthy hermits. While preferences for *risky investments* are relatively low among older adults in the gerontographic clusters, preferences vary considerably for *average-risk investments*. Ailing outgoers is the group least likely to have or aspire to have the latter type of investments. Healthy indulgers is the group most likely to have or express interest in having *low-risk investments*, and healthy hermits is the gerontographic cluster least likely to prefer low-risk investments. Healthy indulgers appear to be the gerontographic segment most receptive to financial services. Older adults in this group show relatively higher preferences for all services examined.

While there are few differences in use of credit cards among older adults possessing different gerontographic characteristics, frail recluses are more likely than healthy hermits to use gasoline cards (Table 5.7).

Purchasing Methods

Preferences for methods of purchasing financial services vary across gerontographic segments (Table 5.8). Preference for door-to-door is four times greater among healthy indulgers than among frail recluses. Healthy hermits and ailing outgoers are also more likely than frail recluses to prefer to purchase financial services from door-to-door agents. On the other hand, more healthy hermits and frail recluses than ailing outgoers prefer purchasing financial services by phone. Finally, frail recluses are more likely to prefer purchasing financial services at vendor's facilities than other gerontographic groups.

Preferences for Sources of Information

Gerontographic characteristics are fairly good predictors of preferences for most sources of information regarding new financial services (Table 5.8). Preferences for television or print ads are stronger among healthy hermits than other gerontographic segments. However, healthy indulgers are less likely to prefer receiving news in the mail, in comparison to healthy hermits, ailing outgoers, and frail recluses. On the other hand, healthy indulgers are more likely to prefer to be contacted by phone than ailing outgoers. Finally, healthy hermits are less likely than any other gerontographic group to express preference for learning about new financial services in group meetings or seminars, in comparison to healthy indulgers, ailing outgoers, and frail recluses.

Table 5.8
Purchasing Methods and Sources of Information for Financial Services

Preferences for Methods of Purchasing Financial Services	Healthy Hermits	Healthy Indulgers	Ailing Outgoers	Frail Recluses
Door-to-door (at home or office)	+	+	+	-
Through the mail	+	-	+	-
By phone – you or they call	+	-	-	+
At vendor's facilities	-	-	-	+
Preferences for Sources of Information Regarding New Financial Services				
Prefer to:				
See TV/print ad	+	-	-	-
Receive news in the mail	+	-	+	+
Be contacted by phone	=	+	-	+
Be visited by agent	-	+	+	-
Learn in group meetings or seminars	-	+	+	+

Institutional-Patronage Preferences

Institutional-patronage preferences vary across gerontographic segments depending upon the type of financial services (Table 5.9). Different gerontographic segments tend to show different preferences for banks, credit unions, and AARP as places to have a *savings or checking account*. A larger percentage of frail recluses than healthy indulgers prefers banks for these services. Healthy indulgers and frail recluses are more likely than healthy hermits to patronize credit unions, and ailing outgoers are more likely than healthy hermits to open a savings or checking account through AARP. Several differences in patronage preferences for *CDs* (certificates of deposit) can be noted among gerontographic groups. More frail recluses than ailing outgoers are likely to prefer getting a CD at a commercial bank. Similarly, credit unions are more likely to be preferred by frail recluses than by ailing outgoers. Healthy indulgers are more likely to patronize savings and loan associations than healthy hermits, ailing outgoers, and frail recluses. The best prospective buyers for CDs for stock brokerage companies are ailing outgoers. Frail recluses are far more likely to get a CD through AARP than healthy hermits.

There are distinct patterns of patronage preferences for *money market accounts* among gerontographic groups. Ailing outgoers and frail recluses are prime prospects for money market accounts at commercial banks. Frail recluses are also twice as likely as healthy hermits to turn to savings and loan associations for these products, while a larger percentage of healthy hermits prefers stock

Table 5.9
Institutional-Patronage Preferences for Select Financial Services

Patronage Preferences for:	Healthy Hermits	Healthy Indulgers	Ailing Outgoers	Frail Recluses
Savings/Checking Account				
Commercial bank	+	-	-	+
Credit union	+	+	-	+
Savings and loan association	-	+	-	+
Stock brokerage company	+	+	+	-
AARP	-	+	+	+
Mutual fund company	+	+	+	-
Certificate of Deposit				
Commercial bank	+	+	-	+
Credit union	-	+	-	+
Savings and loan association	-	+	-	+
Stock brokerage company	+	-	+	-
AARP	-	+	+	+
Mutual fund company	+	-	-	-
Money Market Fund				
Commercial bank	-	-	+	+
Credit union	-	+	+	+
Savings and loan association	-	+	+	+
Stock brokerage company	+	+	-	-
AARP	-	-	+	+
Mutual fund company	+	+	-	-
Government Bonds/U.S. T-bills				
Commercial bank	+	-	-	+
Credit union	+	-	-	+
Savings and loan association	-	-	+	+
Stock brokerage company	+	+	-	-
AARP	-	+	+	+
Mutual fund company	-	+	-	+
Stocks				
Commercial bank	-	-	+	+
Credit union	-	-	+	+
Savings and loan association	-	-	+	-
Stock brokerage company	+	+	-	-
AARP	-	-	+	+
Mutual fund company	+	-	-	-

Table 5.9 (Continued)

Patronage Preferences for:	Healthy Hermits	Healthy Indulgers	Ailing Outgoers	Frail Recluses
IRA/Keogh				
Commercial bank	-	-	+	+
Credit union	+	-	-	+
Savings and loan association	-	+	-	+
Stock brokerage company	+	+	+	-
AARP	-	+	+	+
Mutual fund company	+	+	-	-
Financial Planning				
Commercial bank	-	+	+	+
Credit union	-	-	+	+
Savings and loan association	-	-	+	+
Stock brokerage company	+	+	-	+
AARP	-	-	+	+
Mutual fund company	-	+	-	+
Asset Management Services				
Commercial bank	-	-	+	+
Credit union	-	-	+	+
Savings and loan association	-	-	+	+
Stock brokerage company	+	-	+	-
AARP	+	+	+	-
Mutual fund company	+	+	-	-
Tax Advice				
Commercial bank	-	+	+	+
Credit union	-	+	-	+
Savings and loan association	-	+	-	+
Stock brokerage company	+	+	+	-
AARP	-	+	+	+
Mutual fund company	+	-	-	-
Insurance Policies				
Commercial bank	-	-	+	+
Credit union	-	-	-	+
Savings and loan association	-	-	+	+
Stock brokerage company	+	+	-	-
AARP	-	-	+	-
Mutual fund company	-	+	-	+

brokerage companies than frail recluses or ailing outgoers. Frail recluses are the best prospects for having a money market account from AARP. Healthy hermits are more likely than ailing outgoers to patronize mutual fund companies for money market accounts.

Gerontographic segments favor different types of financial institutions for *government bonds* and *United States Treasury bills*. Commercial banks are more likely to be preferred by frail recluses than ailing outgoers. A significantly greater percentage of ailing outgoers and frail recluses than healthy hermits is likely to prefer savings and loan associations for these financial products. A larger proportion of healthy hermits than ailing outgoers is likely to patronize stock brokerage firms. Healthy hermits are less likely than any of the remaining gerontographic groups to purchase government bonds and U.S. Treasury bills from AARP. Finally, healthy indulgers and frail recluses are more likely than ailing outgoers to prefer mutual fund companies for these financial services.

More frail recluses and ailing outgoers than healthy hermits and healthy indulgers are likely to prefer commercial banks as places from which to purchase *stocks*. Ailing outgoers are relatively more likely than frail recluses to patronize savings and loan associations. Stock brokerage companies are favored more by healthy hermits and healthy indulgers than ailing outgoers. On the other hand, ailing outgoers are more likely than the two former groups to prefer buying stocks through AARP. Finally, healthy hermits are more likely than ailing outgoers to patronize mutual fund companies when they buy stocks.

Frail recluses appear to be the best prospects of traditional financial institutions for *IRA/Keogh* plans. More of them would turn to a commercial bank, in comparison to healthy hermits, healthy indulgers, and ailing outgoers. Similarly, frail recluses are twice as likely as healthy indulgers to patronize credit unions for IRA or Keogh plans. More frail recluses prefer to deal with savings and loan associations than healthy hermits and ailing outgoers. Finally, frail recluses are more likely than healthy hermits to seek IRA/Keogh plans through AARP. On the other hand, frail recluses are less likely than mature consumers in other gerontographic segments to patronize stock brokerage companies. Mutual fund companies are more popular among healthy indulgers than among ailing outgoers and frail recluses, while healthy hermits are more likely than ailing outgoers to show preferences for mutual fund companies for IRA/Keogh plans.

Healthy hermits are not as likely as older adults of other gerontographic characteristics to go to commercial banks for *financial-planning services*. Frail recluses are more likely than healthy hermits to prefer credit unions for these services. Similarly, savings and loans are favored more by frail recluses and ailing outgoers than by healthy hermits. Finally, a larger proportion of ailing outgoers than healthy indulgers and healthy hermits would prefer to receive financial-planning services from AARP.

The older person's gerontographic characteristic is likely to predict patronage preferences for *asset-management services*. Commercial banks are mostly favored by frail recluses than any other gerontographic group. Healthy hermits are less likely to prefer banks than frail recluses and ailing outgoers. Ailing outgoers, on the other hand, are more likely than any other group to prefer savings and loan associations for asset-management services. Healthy hermits favor stock brokerage companies more than healthy indulgers, ailing outgoers, and frail recluses. Healthy hermits and healthy indulgers are more likely than ailing outgoers to prefer mutual fund companies for asset-management services.

The older person's gerontographic profile is likely to predict his or her preferences for receiving *tax advice* from various types of financial institutions. Specifically, close to one-fourth of healthy indulgers, in comparison to higher percentages of ailing outgoers and frail recluses, prefers receiving tax advice from commercial banks. Similarly, frail recluses are twice as likely as healthy hermits to seek advice on taxes from credit unions. However, frail recluses are less likely to turn to stock brokerage companies for tax advice than older adults in other gerontographic groups. Finally, healthy hermits are less likely than other groups to prefer AARP as a source of advice on taxes.

Patronage preferences for purchasing *insurance* services from nontraditional providers show variation across gerontographic groups. Ailing outgoers and frail recluses are more likely than healthy hermits to prefer commercial banks for insurance services. Frail recluses are more likely than other groups to favor credit unions for insurance policies. Frail recluses are more likely than healthy hermits and healthy indulgers to prefer savings and loan associations as vendors for insurance services. However, a larger percentage of healthy hermits than frail recluses is likely to prefer stock brokerage firms as a nontraditional source from which to buy insurance services. Finally, ailing outgoers are more likely than healthy hermits to prefer purchasing insurance from AARP.

Patronage Motives

The older person's gerontographic profile appears to be a good indicator of his or her inclination to take certain factors into consideration in patronage decisions (Table 5.10). Only the importance of billing methods, fees charged by financial institutions, and referrals are not likely to vary across gerontographic clusters. Nearly half of healthy indulgers think that convenience in reaching the service provider is important in patronage decisions. Ease of getting related services at the same place is of greater importance to healthy indulgers than to any other gerontographic group. Explanation of various services by staff or personnel is mostly valued by healthy indulgers and frail recluses. The latter group is also more likely to need assistance with filling out forms than healthy hermits. Frail recluses and healthy hermits are also likely to differ with respect to the importance they place on senior discounts, with a larger percentage of the former group than of the latter group citing this reason.

While only a small percentage of older Americans considers the way older people are portrayed in ads, a larger percentage of ailing outgoers than healthy hermits or frail recluses cites this reason to be an important patronage motive.

Table 5.10
Reasons for Patronizing Financial Institutions

Reasons for patronizing	Healthy Hermits	Healthy Indulgers	Ailing Outgoers	Frail Recluses
Reasonable prices or fees	-	+	-	+
Convenience in reaching the service provider	-	+	-	+
Ease of getting related services at the same place	-	+	+	+
Explanation of various services by staff/personnel	-	+	-	+
Personnel/staff assistance with filling out forms	-	+	+	+
Discounts to age groups (children, seniors)	-	-	+	+
Preference for billing/payment methods	-	+	-	+
You like the way their ads show people your age	-	+	+	-
Special deals through group or membership programs	-	+	+	+
Advice of children or close relatives	-	-	+	-
Advice of other people your age	-	-	+	-
Referrals/endorsements by firms or professionals	-	+	+	-
Ease of doing business by phone or by mail	-	+	-	+

Advice of family members on patronage decisions concerning financial institutions has a strong influence on ailing outgoers. Similarly, ailing outgoers are more receptive to special deals through membership programs than healthy hermits. These two groups also differ with regard to word-of-mouth communication from peers of similar age. Finally, healthy indulgers are more likely to value the convenience of doing business by phone or mail in comparison to healthy hermits and ailing outgoers.

Asset Composition

Asset composition also varies by gerontographic characteristics of older Americans. A larger percentage of healthy hermits than frail recluses and healthy indulgers reports liquid assets in excess of $50,000. About half of healthy hermits and ailing outgoers in comparison to frail recluses and healthy indulgers report investments in securities in excess of $5,000. Tangible assets are widely held by ailing outgoers, with nearly nine in ten expressing values in such assets in excess of $5,000, in comparison to three-fourths of frail recluses. Seven in

Table 5.11
Preferences for Using Various Types of Investments to Pay Post-Retirement Expenses

Types of Investments & Expenses	Healthy Hermits	Healthy Indulgers	Ailing Outgoers	Frail Recluses
Use IRA/KEOGH, Pension to Pay:				
Large, unexpected medical bills	-	+	-	+
Vacation/Travel	-	+	-	+
Home improvements	-	+	-	+
Nursing home or long-term care	-	+	-	+
Gifts to relatives and charities	-	+	-	+
Major purchases, such as cars and furniture	-	+	-	+
Personal and business investments	-	+	-	+
Use Home Equity to Pay:				
Large, unexpected medical bills	+	+	-	+
Vacation/Travel	=	-	-	+
Home improvements	-	+	-	+
Nursing home or long-term care	+	-	-	+
Gifts to relatives and charities	+	-	-	+
Major purchases, such as cars and furniture	-	+	-	+
Personal and business investments	-	-	+	+
Use Other Investments to Pay:				
Large, unexpected medical bills	-	+	-	+
Vacation/Travel	-	+	-	+
Home improvements	-	+	-	+
Nursing home or long-term care	-	+	-	+
Gifts to relatives and charities	-	+	-	+
Major purchases, such as cars and furniture	-	+	-	+
Personal and business investments	-	+	-	+

ten ailing outgoers, substantially more than frail recluses and healthy hermits, report real estate equities in excess of $50,000. Finally, frail recluses own the least in ''other'' assets.

Use of Investments

Use of various types of investments depends on the older person's gerontographic profile (Table 5.11). The older person's gerontographic profile provides a good indication of his or her preferences for using income from *IRA/Keogh or pension* to pay for various post-retirement expenses. Healthy indulgers and frail recluses are more likely than healthy hermits to favor the use of IRA/Keogh or pension funds to pay for large medical bills. Healthy indulgers and frail recluses are also more likely than their older counterparts in other gerontographic groups to use these savings for travel and leisure, home improvements, nursing home or long-term care, gifts, major purchases, and personal and business investments.

The older person's gerontographic characteristics are good predictors of his or her attitudes toward use of *home equity* to pay for several expenses after retirement. A larger percentage of healthy indulgers and frail recluses than healthy hermits and ailing outgoers favor use of home equity for home improvements after retirement. Twice as many frail recluses as ailing outgoers and healthy indulgers favor use of home equity to pay for nursing home or long-term care expenses after retirement. Twice as many ailing outgoers as healthy hermits think that home equity should be used for personal and business investments. Finally, a larger percentage of frail recluses than healthy indulgers recommends use of home equity by retirees to pay for vacation and travel expenses.

The older person's gerontographic profile is a rather good indicator of his or her opinion on how older people should spend *"other" investments*. Frail recluses are more likely than older adults in other gerontographic groups to express the desire for spending these assets on large, unexpected medical bills. Wide variations in preferences for spending on vacation/travel also exists, with a relatively larger percentage of healthy indulgers than ailing outgoers and healthy hermits expressing preferences for spending on leisure. Also, relatively larger numbers of healthy indulgers and frail recluses than healthy hermits are likely to favor spending investment assets on home improvements. A larger percentage of frail recluses than any other gerontographic segment is likely to feel the need for spending these assets on nursing home or long-term care. Healthy indulgers are more likely than any other group to prefer spending on gifts and donations to charities. Frail recluses and healthy indulgers are more likely than healthy hermits and ailing outgoers to prefer spending investment assets on major purchases such as cars and furniture, as well as putting these resources in other types of personal and business investments.

Home Equity

While preferences for the majority of methods for tapping one's home equity do not differ across gerontographic segments, two methods show significant differences (Table 5.12). Specifically, a larger percentage of frail recluses and healthy indulgers than healthy hermits is likely to prefer receiving all the cash now and making monthly payments to the lender. The same groups also are the most and least likely, respectively, to prefer getting money out of their home equity by selling their present home and buying a less expensive one.

Table 5.12
Preferences for Methods of Getting Cash from Home Equity

Methods/Options	Healthy Hermits	Healthy Indulgers	Ailing Outgoers	Frail Recluses
Receive all the cash now and you make monthly payments to the lender	-	+	-	+
Sell your home, but continue to live there and receive small monthly payments from the new owner	+	=	-	+
Sell your present home, rent another home, and keep all the cash	+	-	+	-
Sell your present home, buy a less expensive home, and keep the cash difference	-	+	+	+
Receive all the cash now and the lender gets your home when you move or die	+	-	+	-
Receive monthly cash payment and the lender gets your home when you move or die	-	+	+	-

HIGH-TECH PRODUCTS AND TELECOMMUNICATION SERVICES

Preference for Products and Services

The older person's gerontographic characteristics are strong predictors of his or her preference for high-tech and telecommunication products and services (Table 5.13). While four in ten healthy indulgers own a telephone-answering machine, ownership/use of this product among the other gerontographic groups is less than three in ten. Ownership of home-security systems, on the other hand, is twice as high among frail recluses and healthy indulgers as it is among healthy hermits. Finally, a significantly larger percentage of frail recluses and healthy indulgers than healthy hermits and ailing outgoers owns energy-saving appliances or installed devices. Gerontographics are very strong predictors of new automobile purchases. Healthy indulgers is the group most likely to report ownership of a 5-year-old (or more recent) model, with more than eight in ten of them indicating present ownership.

Turning to preferences for telecommunication services, the gerontographic groups differ significantly with respect to the three services examined. Ailing outgoers, healthy indulgers, and frail recluses prefer operator-assisted services the most, with about two-thirds of mature adults in these groups indicating

Table 5.13
Purchase and Consumption of High-Tech Products and Telecommunication Services

Preferences for High-Tech Products and Telecommunication Services	Healthy Hermits	Healthy Indulgers	Ailing Outgoers	Frail Recluses
Use of High-Tech products				
Home-security system	-	+	-	+
Telephone-answering machine	-	+	-	+
Energy-saving appliances or installed devices	-	+	-	+
A five year old or more recent model of automobile	-	+	-	+
Services				
Operator-assisted services (such as directory assistance)	-	+	+	+
Operator-assisted service that locates people you have lost touch with	-	-	+	-
Discount or "package" long-distance telephone plan	-	+	+	+
Preferences for Sources of Information Regarding New Electronic Products				
Prefer to:				
See TV/print ad	-	+	-	+
Receive news in the mail	+	-	+	-
Be contacted by phone	-	+	+	-
Be visited by agent	-	-	+	+
Learn in group meetings or seminars	-	+	+	-

preference for such services. The same three groups also are likely to be the heaviest users of discount or "package" long-distance telephone plans, with nearly half of ailing outgoers expressing preference, in comparison to slightly more than one-third of healthy hermits.

Preferences for Sources of Information

The older person's gerontographic characteristic is a strong predictor of his or her preference for sources of consumer information regarding electronic products (Table 5.13). Nearly two-thirds of frail recluses, in comparison to less than half of ailing outgoers, prefer to see television or print ads of new electronic products. One in three of healthy hermits and ailing outgoers, in comparison to approximately one in four of older adults in the other gerontographic groups, prefers to receive news in the mail. Frail recluses is the group most likely to prefer an agent's visit, although the incidence of preference for this source is rather low. Finally, a larger percentage of ailing outgoers than healthy hermits and frail recluses prefers to hear about new electronic products in group meetings or seminars.

The older person's gerontographic profile can predict the type of information source he or she may prefer for new telecommunication services, in relation to older adults having other gerontographic profiles (Table 5.14). A larger percentage of frail recluses, in comparison to healthy indulgers, prefers receiving news in the mail about telecommunication services. Frail recluses are also more likely than healthy hermits to prefer to be visited by an agent. Finally, more ailing outgoers and healthy indulgers than frail recluses prefer hearing news about new telecommunication services in group meetings or seminars.

Payment Systems

Gerontographic characteristics predict the older person's preference for certain types of payment systems in the case of burglar or fire alarm system purchases (Table 5.14). Although there are no significant differences in preferences for cash as a method of payment for these products, a larger percentage of frail recluses than healthy indulgers prefers checks as a payment method. One in four of frail recluses, in comparison to less than one in five among healthy indulgers and ailing outgoers, would use a credit card. Coupons are more likely to be used by ailing outgoers than by healthy indulgers. Finally, senior/member discounts are more likely to be used by frail recluses and ailing outgoers than by the remaining gerontographic groups.

The older persons' gerontographic characteristics predict their preferences for payment methods regarding home-appliance repair services (Table 5.14). Frail recluses are somewhat more likely than ailing outgoers to prefer using cash. Nearly one in five of healthy hermits and frail recluses, in comparison to slightly more than one in ten of ailing outgoers, prefers credit cards, and healthy indulgers are less likely to use coupons than any other gerontographic group. Finally, ailing outgoers is the group most likely to prefer senior/member discounts, while healthy indulgers prefer these offerings the least.

Purchasing Methods

Gerontographic characteristics of older consumers predict preferences for certain types of distribution methods for purchasing electronic products (Table 5.15). While the incidence of purchasing electronic products door-to-door is very

Table 5.14
Preferences for Sources of Information and Payment Methods

Preferences for Sources of Information Regarding New Telecommunication Services	Healthy Hermits	Healthy Indulgers	Ailing Outgoers	Frail Recluses
Prefer to:				
See TV/print ad	=	+	-	+
Receive news in the mail	-	-	=	+
Be contacted by phone	+	+	-	-
Be visited by agent	-	+	-	+
Learn in group meetings or seminars	-	+	+	-
Preferences for Payment Methods for Burglar or Fire Alarm System				
Cash	+	-	-	-
Check	-	-	+	+
Credit Card	+	-	-	+
Coupon	+	-	+	+
Senior/member discount	-	-	+	+
Preferences for Payment Methods for Home-Appliance Repair Services				
Cash	-	+	-	+
Check	-	-	-	+
Credit card	+	-	-	+
Coupon	+	-	+	+
Senior/member discount	-	-	+	+

small, older Americans who prefer this method are more likely to be healthy indulgers than healthy hermits or frail recluses. Healthy indulgers, however, are less likely than healthy hermits to buy through the mail. But healthy hermits are less likely than frail recluses to buy at vendor's facilities.

Reasons for Buying Direct

Older consumers do not consider each of the eight factors equally in buying electronic products direct (Table 5.15). The older person's likelihood of considering most of the factors examined appears to be influenced by his/her geron-

Table 5.15
Preferences for Methods of Purchasing Electronic Products

Preferences for Methods of Purchasing Electronic Products	Healthy Hermits	Healthy Indulgers	Ailing Outgoers	Frail Recluses
Door-to-door (at home or office)	-	+	+	-
Through the mail	+	-	-	+
By phone -- you or they call	+	+	-	-
At vendor's facilities	-	-	-	+
Reasons Considered Before Buying Electronic Products by Phone or Through the Mail				
Price (including shipping charges)	-	+	-	-
Type of credit card accepted	-	+	-	+
Return/cancellation and refund policy	-	+	+	+
Convenience, in comparison to other ways of buying the same product/service	+	+	-	-
Free pick-up service for returns	-	+	+	+
Availability of toll free (800) number	-	-	+	+
Selection of products or services	-	+	-	+
Days to wait before receiving	-	+	-	+

tographic profile. About one-third of frail recluses, in comparison to one in four of healthy hermits, indicates they would consider type of credit card accepted. Convenience, in relation to alternative methods of buying electronic products, is of greater importance to healthy indulgers than to any other gerontographic group. Free pick-up service for returns is important to more than one-third of healthy hermits, in comparison to the remaining gerontographic groups, in which nearly four in ten consider this service before buying direct. Availability of a toll-free number is of greater importance to frail recluses than to healthy hermits.

HEALTH-CARE PRODUCTS AND SERVICES

Gerontographic characteristics are very strong predictors of the older person's level of concern with various types of health problems. Since gerontographic characteristics are based in part on the older person's health status, it is not surprising that they predict rather accurately his or her concern with a number of health problems. Generally speaking, ailing outgoers are those most con-

Table 5.16
Purchase and Consumption of Health-Care Products and Services

Products Owned/Used	Healthy Hermits	Healthy Indulgers	Ailing Outgoers	Frail Recluses
Exercise equipment (at home)	-	+	-	+
Prescription drug for chronic condition	-	-	+	-
Dietary meal prescription or products for people with certain health/physical requirements	-	-	+	-
Self-diagnostic medical equipment (at home)	-	-	+	+
Preferences for Health-Care Services				
Health club membership	-	+	+	-
Paid at-home assistance with personal needs and chores	-	+	+	-
Low-cost health-membership program providing free or discounted rates for services in areas that concern you	-	-	+	+
Medical care services provided at your home	-	+	+	+
Preferences for Sources of Information Regarding New Health Care Services				
Prefer to:				
See TV/print ad	+	+	-	-
Receive news in the mail	-	-	+	+
Be contacted by phone	-	+	-	-
Be visited by agent	-	-	+	-
Learn in group meetings or seminars	-	+	+	-

cerned with the various health-related problems; healthy hermits are those least concerned, with the remaining two groups falling in between.

Use of Products and Services

Gerontographic characteristics predict ownership/use of all five products examined (Table 5.16). Use of prescription drugs is higher among ailing outgoers than any other gerontographic group. Ailing outgoers are also more likely than healthy hermits and healthy indulgers to report usage of products for people with certain health/physical requirements. Frail recluses are about twice as likely as older adults in the remaining gerontographic groups to report ownership/use of self-diagnostic medical equipment; they are also more likely than any other group to report use/ownership of exercise equipment, with half of them reporting ownership/usage. Finally, healthy indulgers and ailing outgoers make heavier use of hair-care and face-care products than their counterparts in the remaining gerontographic groups.

Gerontographics are very strong determinants of the older person's preferences for the four types of health-care services examined (Table 5.16). Membership in health clubs is higher among ailing outgoers and healthy indulgers, with more than one-fourth of older adults in these gerontographic groups indicating use or desire for this service. Paid at-home assistance is most valuable to healthy indulgers, with over one-third of older adults in this group expressing preference. Three in ten of ailing outgoers are likely to prefer receiving assistance with personal needs and chores for a fee, in comparison to two in ten of healthy hermits.

Frail recluses are a prime target for health-membership programs, with two in three expressing preference. On the other hand, healthy hermits are least likely to favor these programs, with only four in ten expressing preference. Ailing outgoers are also prime prospects for health-membership programs. Half of the healthy indulgers are likely to express preference for health-membership programs.

Finally, one in two frail recluses is likely to indicate preference for receiving medical-care services at their home, in comparison to nearly one in three healthy hermits. The two remaining groups are also likely to be prime prospects, with more than one in four of individuals in these groups likely to express preferences for receiving medical-care services at their home.

Preferences for Sources of Information

Not all gerontographic segments prefer to learn about new health-care services from the same sources (Table 5.16). A somewhat larger percentage of healthy hermits and healthy indulgers than of ailing outgoers prefers to see the information on television or print ads. Frail recluses is the group most likely to prefer receiving news in the mail, in comparison to healthy indulgers, who are the group least likely to prefer this source. Ailing outgoers are also likely to prefer this source. Ailing outgoers are more likely than healthy hermits to prefer an agent's call for information about new health-care services.

Reasons for Patronizing Hospitals

The older person's gerontographic profile explains nearly every patronage reason when it comes to choosing among hospitals (Table 5.17). First, with respect to the importance of fees charged for health-care services, ailing outgoers

Table 5.17
Reasons for Patronizing Specific Hospitals

Reasons for Patronizing	Healthy Hermits	Healthy Indulgers	Ailing Outgoers	Frail Recluses
Reasonable prices or fees	-	-	+	+
Convenience in reaching the service provider	+	=	-	-
Ease of getting related services at the same place	+	+	+	-
Explanation of various services by staff/personnel	-	+	+	-
Personnel/staff assistance with filling out forms	-	+	+	+
Discounts to age groups (children, seniors)	-	-	+	+
Preference for billing/payment methods	-	-	+	+
You like the way their ads show people your age	-	+	+	−
Special deals through group or membership programs	-	-	+	+
Advice of children or close relatives	-	-	+	-
Advice of other people your age	-	+	+	-
Referrals/endorsements by firms or professionals	-	+	-	-
Ease of doing business by phone or by mail	+	-	+	-

are nearly twice as likely as healthy hermits to value low fees/prices charged by hospitals. A larger percentage of healthy indulgers than frail recluses values the importance of getting other health-care services at the same place. A larger percentage of healthy indulgers than frail recluses and healthy hermits would patronize a hospital because of staff/personnel willingness to explain various health-care services.

Ailing outgoers are twice as likely as healthy hermits to consider the availability of senior discounts. Also, ailing outgoers and frail recluses are more concerned with the types of payment or billing methods available than older adults in the remaining gerontographic groups. Ailing outgoers are more likely than other gerontographic groups to patronize hospitals because they like the way hospital ads show people their own age; and they are more likely than healthy hermits to value special deals through group or membership programs. While advice of children or close relatives is not reported by older Americans to be a determinant patronage reason, a larger percentage of ailing outgoers is likely to rely on such advice, in comparison to healthy hermits. Ailing outgoers are more likely than frail recluses to consider ability of doing business by phone or by mail in their patronage decisions concerning hospitals and clinics. Finally, healthy indulgers are more likely than older adults in the remaining geronto- graphic groups to rely on referrals in choosing a hospital. They are also more likely than healthy hermits to rely on advice from people their own age, with nearly one in four indicating this to be an important patronage reason.

Reasons for Selecting Physicians and Surgeons

Gerontographic characteristics of older adults are very strong predictors of the types of criteria mature patients will rely upon in selecting physicians and surgeons (Table 5.18). A larger percentage of ailing outgoers than older adults in other gerontographic groups is likely to select health-care professionals on the basis of the fees they charge for their services. On the other hand, ailing outgoers and healthy hermits are less likely than frail recluses to choose health- care professionals on the basis of convenience.

A larger percentage of healthy indulgers than healthy hermits and frail re- cluses patronizes certain physicians and surgeons because these professionals satisfactorily explain the various health-care services to them. Healthy indulgers are also more likely than healthy hermits to value assistance offered in filling out forms. Senior discounts as patronage incentives are of greatest appeal to ailing outgoers and least appealing to healthy hermits. Ailing outgoers and frail recluses are more likely than older adults in other gerontographic groups to consider the various billing/payment options available to them; and the former two groups are more likely than healthy hermits to like the way people their age are portrayed in advertisements by health-care professionals. Membership programs are likely to be of greater appeal to frail recluses than to healthy hermits.

Advice of children or close relatives is of greater influence on ailing outgoers than on any other gerontographic group, as well as the advice of other people of the same age. Finally, ailing outgoers are more likely to value the convenience of doing business by phone or by mail than older adults in other gerontographic groups.

Payment Methods

Gerontographic characteristics are good predictors of preferences for certain methods of payment for health-care services (Table 5.19). Frail recluses and healthy hermits are more likely to prefer paying cash for health-care services than ailing outgoers. Frail recluses are also more likely than ailing outgoers to

Table 5.18
Reasons for Patronizing Specific Physicians and Surgeons

Reasons for Patronizing	Healthy Hermits	Healthy Indulgers	Ailing Outgoers	Frail Recluses
Reasonable prices or fees	-	-	+	-
Convenience in reaching the service provider	-	+	-	+
Ease of getting related services at the same place	+	-	-	-
Explanation of various services by staff/personnel	-	+	+	-
Personnel/staff assistance with filling out forms	-	+	+	+
Discounts to age groups (children, seniors)	-	+	+	+
Preference for billing/payment methods	-	-	+	+
You like the way their ads show people your age	-	+	+	+
Special deals through group or membership programs	-	+	+	+
Advice of children or close relatives	-	-	+	-
Advice of other people your age	-	+	+	-
Referrals/endorsements by firms or professionals	-	+	+	+
Ease of doing business by phone or by mail	-	-	+	-

prefer paying by credit card. However, both frail recluses and ailing outgoers are more likely than the remaining gerontographic groups to take advantage of senior/member discounts.

Gerontographic characteristics offer additional input into the description of older adults' preferences for payment of eyeglasses (Table 5.19). A larger percentage of frail recluses than ailing outgoers and healthy hermits prefers payment by cash. A larger percentage of frail recluses than healthy indulgers and ailing outgoers prefers checks as a form of payment for eyeglasses purchased at optical centers. Credit card preference is higher among healthy indulgers than among ailing outgoers. Finally, senior/member discounts are preferred more by frail recluses and ailing outgoers than by older adults in the remaining gerontographic groups.

Table 5.19
Preferences for Methods of Payment for Health-Care Services and Products

Care Services	Healthy Hermits	Healthy Indulgers	Ailing Outgoers	Frail Recluses
Cash	+	-	-	+
Check	-	+	+	+
Credit Card	+	-	-	+
Coupon	-	-	+	+
Senior/member discount	-	-	+	+
Eye Glasses				
Cash	-	+	-	+
Check	=	-	-	+
Credit Card	+	+	-	+
Coupon	+	-	+	+
Senior/member discount	-	-	+	+

INSURANCE SERVICES

Preferences for Services

Preferences for various types of insurance policies vary across gerontographic groups (Table 5.20). Healthy hermits are less likely to prefer various insurance products, except car insurance, than any other gerontographic group. The remaining groups do not differ greatly in their preferences. Ailing outgoers are more likely than frail recluses to have or express desire for "medigap."

Preferences for Sources of Information

Gerontographic characteristics of older adults predict preferences for two types of information sources regarding new insurance products (Table 5.20). First, those who prefer to hear about new insurance products from sales agents are more likely to be healthy indulgers than either frail recluses or ailing outgoers. However, ailing outgoers are twice as likely as healthy indulgers and healthy hermits to want to learn about new insurance services in group meetings or seminars.

Table 5.20
Preferences for Insurance Services

Preferences for Insurance Services	Healthy Hermits	Healthy Indulgers	Ailing Outgoers	Frail Recluses
Long-term care insurance (besides Medicare/Medicaid)	-	+	+	+
Health insurance that supplements Medicare ("Medigap")	-	-	+	-
Car insurance	-	+	-	-
Home health-care insurance (besides Medicare/Medicaid)	-	=	+	+
Preferences for Sources of Information Regarding New Insurance Services				
Prefer to:				
See TV/print ad	+	+	-	+
Receive news in the mail	=	-	+	+
Be contacted by phone	-	+	+	+
Be visited by agent	+	+	-	-
Learn in group meetings or seminars	-	-	+	+
Patronage Preferences for Insurance Policies				
Commercial bank	-	-	+	+
Credit union	-	-	-	+
Savings and loan Association	-	-	+	+
Stock brokerage co.	+	=	-	-
AARP	-	-	+	-
Mutual fund co.	-	+	-	+

Institutional Patronage

Gerontographic characteristics can predict the older person's patronage preferences for insurance products (Table 5.20). Commercial banks are most likely to be preferred by ailing outgoers and frail recluses. Credit unions are preferred mostly by frail recluses; they are also more likely to be patronized by ailing outgoers than by healthy hermits and healthy indulgers. Stock brokerage companies are more likely to be patronized by healthy hermits than by frail recluses.

Table 5.21
Reasons for Patronizing Insurance Companies

Reasons for Patronizing Insurance Companies	Healthy Hermits	Healthy Indulgers	Ailing Outgoers	Frail Recluses
Reasonable prices or fees	-	-	+	-
Convenience in reaching the service provider	-	+	+	-
Ease of getting related services at the same place	-	+	+	-
Explanation of various services by staff/personnel	-	+	+	-
Personnel/staff assistance with filling out forms	-	+	+	-
Discounts to age groups (children, seniors)	-	+	+	-
Preference for billing/payment methods	-	+	+	+
You like the way their ads show people your age	-	+	+	-
Special deals through group or membership programs	-	-	+	-
Advice of children or close relatives	-	-	+	-
Advice of other people your age	-	-	+	+
Referrals/endorsements by firms or professionals	-	+	+	-
Ease of doing business by phone or by mail	=	+	+	-

Patronage Reasons

The gerontographic profiles of older Americans are very good predictors of the type of factors they would consider before choosing an insurance-service provider to buy various types of insurance services (Table 5.21). Prices of various policies are most likely to be considered by ailing outgoers than any other gerontographic group. Ailing outgoers are also more likely than healthy hermits to consider convenience in reaching the service provider. The same appears to be the case with respect to ease of getting related services at the same place, personnel assistance with filling out forms, age-based discounts, preferences for billing methods, portrayal of the older spokespersons in ads, special deals through group or special programs, advice of family members, and referrals or endorsements by firms or professionals.

Table 5.22
Purchase of Insurance Services

Preferences for Method of Purchasing Insurance Services	Healthy Hermits	Healthy Indulgers	Ailing Outgoers	Frail Recluses
Door-to-door (at home or office)	-	+	+	-
Through the mail	-	-	+	-
By phone -- you or they call	+	-	+	+
At vendor's facilities	-	+	-	+
Reasons Considered Before Buying Various Types of Insurance by Phone or Through the Mail				
Price (including shipping charges)	-	-	+	+
Type of credit card accepted	-	+	+	-
Return/cancellation and refund policy	-	-	+	-
Convenience, in comparison to other ways of buying the same product/service	-	-	+	-
Free pick-up service for returns	+	-	+	-
Availability of toll free (800) number	-	-	+	+
Selection of products or services	-	+	+	-
Days to wait before receiving	-	-	+	-

Ailing outgoers are also more likely than frail recluses to value the ease of getting related services at the same place, personnel/staff assistance with filling out forms, age-based discounts, portrayals of older spokespersons in ads, special deals through group or membership programs, advice of relatives, referrals/endorsements by firms or professionals, and ease of doing business by phone or by mail. Finally, healthy indulgers are more likely than healthy hermits to value personnel/staff assistance with filling out forms and to consider portrayals of older spokespersons in advertisements.

Purchasing Methods

Preferences for methods of buying insurance policies are likely to differ among older adults in various gerontographic groups (Table 5.22). One-third of healthy indulgers, compared to a smaller percentage of healthy hermits and frail recluses, prefers buying insurance policies from salespeople door-to-door. Ailing outgoers are more likely than healthy indulgers to prefer buying through the mail. However, healthy indulgers are those least likely to prefer the phone as a method of buying insurance. Frail recluses prefer purchasing these services at vendor's facilities more than any other group, while ailing outgoers are the group least likely to prefer this mode of distribution.

Reasons for Buying Direct

Gerontographic groups do differ in the way they respond to a number of factors related to direct buying (Table 5.22). Ailing outgoers and frail recluses pay more attention to price than healthy hermits and healthy indulgers. Ailing outgoers are twice as likely as frail recluses to consider the type(s) of credit card(s) accepted. Also, ailing outgoers are more likely than the remaining groups to consider cancellation and refund policies. Nearly half of frail recluses would consider the availability of a toll-free phone number, in comparison to a smaller percentage of healthy indulgers and healthy hermits.

Preference for Long-Term Care Insurance

The person's gerontographic profile appears to be the best predictor of his or her willingness to purchase *long-term care insurance* (Table 5.23). While freedom to choose the place and type of care is of greater value to all groups except the healthy hermits, there are variations in willingness to pay for coverage of the remaining services. Ailing outgoers are more likely than any other group to express willingness to pay, with half of them expressing interest, in comparison to a much smaller percentage of frail recluses, healthy indulgers, and healthy hermits. Ailing outgoers are also more likely to pay for home-health and personal care than older adults with other gerontographic profiles. Ailing outgoers are more likely to value companion or monitoring services, with four in five of them expressing interest, in comparison to about one in three healthy hermits and one in four frail recluses. Similarly, more than half of ailing outgoers would pay to insure themselves for nutrition and preventive health-care programs they might need, in comparison to about one-third of older adults in the remaining gerontographic groups.

Ailing outgoers are nearly twice as likely as frail recluses to express interest in paying for insurance now for future benefits that would cover legal and tax advice. They are also more likely than any other group to pay for adult day care and transportation or escort services. They are twice as likely as frail recluses to pay now to ensure they will have someone later in life to manage their finances and help them pay bills.

There are also significant differences in preferences for using supplemental or long-term care insurance by gerontographic groups. A larger percentage of healthy indulgers, in comparison to healthy hermits, frail recluses, and ailing

Table 5.23
Interest in Purchasing and Using Long-Term Care Insurance

Willingness to Pay for Long-Term Care Insurance that Would Provide Oneself the Benefits of:	Healthy Hermits	Healthy Indulgers	Ailing Outgoers	Frail Recluses
Freedom to choose place and type of care	-	+	+	+
Housekeeping and chores	+	-	+	-
Home health and personal care	-	-	+	-
Companion or monitoring services	-	+	+	-
Nutrition and preventive health-care programs	-	-	+	-
Legal and tax advice	-	-	+	-
Adult day care	-	-	+	-
Transportation or escort services	=	-	+	-
Money management and bill payment	-	-	+	-
Use of Supplemental Long-Term Care Insurance to Pay for:				
Large, unexpected medical bills	-	+	-	-
Nursing home or long-term care	+	+	-	=

outgoers, shows willingness to use supplemental or long-term care insurance to pay for large medical bills. Similarly, healthy indulgers are more likely than any other group to prefer using supplemental or long-term care insurance to pay for nursing home or long-term care expenses. About three-fifths of healthy hermits and frail recluses, and about two-thirds of the healthy indulgers, compared to just over half of ailing outgoers, show preference for using supplemental or long-term care insurance to pay for nursing home or long-term care expenses.

Among those married, gerontographic characteristics are very strong predictors of the older person's propensity to indicate willingness to pay for *long-term care insurance for his or her spouse* (Table 5.24). As in the case with insuring oneself, ailing outgoers are most receptive to long-term care insurance for their spouse, and they are the group most likely to value all the services long-term care insurance covers. Healthy hermits are likely to be less interested than the remaining groups in paying for freedom to choose the place and type of care their spouse might need. However, healthy hermits are more likely than healthy indulgers and frail recluses to pay for housekeeping and chores, and for tax and legal advice benefits their spouse might need in the future.

Of those with living parent(s), a much larger percentage of ailing outgoers

Table 5.24
Interest in Purchasing LTC Insurance for Spouse and Parent(s)

Willingness to Pay for Long-Term Care Insurance that Would Provide Spouse the Benefits of:	Healthy Hermits	Healthy Indulgers	Ailing Outgoers	Frail Recluses
Freedom to choose place and type of care	-	+	+	+
Housekeeping and chores	-	-	+	-
Home health and personal care	-	-	+	-
Companion or monitoring services	-	-	+	-
Nutrition and preventive health-care programs	-	-	+	-
Legal and tax advice	+	-	+	-
Adult day care	-	-	+	-
Transportation or escort services	-	-	+	-
Money management and bill payment	-	-	+	-
Willingness to Provide for Long-Term Care Insurance that Would Provide Parent(s) the Benefits of:				
Freedom to choose place and type of care	-	-	+	+
Housekeeping and chores	+	-	+	-
Home health and personal care	-	+	+	-
Companion or monitoring services	+	-	-	+
Nutrition and preventive health-care programs	+	-	-	-
Legal and tax advice	+	-	+	-
Adult day care	+	+	+	-
Transportation or escort services	+	-	+	-
Money management and bill payment	+	-	+	-

and frail recluses than healthy hermits is likely to express willingness to pay for *long-term care insurance for their parents'* freedom to choose the place and type of care they want (Table 5.24). However, a significantly greater percentage of healthy hermits than healthy indulgers is willing to pay for insurance now that would cover the cost of housekeeping and assistance with chores for their parents. Healthy hermits are also more concerned with their aged parents' health, with more than one-third of them expressing willingness to pay for this type of coverage, in comparison to frail recluses and healthy indulgers.

Ailing outgoers appear to be more eager to protect their parents in the event they need tax and legal advice. A larger percentage of this group, in comparison to frail recluses and healthy indulgers, is interested in paying now for insurance that would cover assistance with legal and tax matters, if their parents ever need it in the future. Also, a larger percentage of ailing outgoers and healthy hermits than frail recluses is willing to pay for transportation or escort services their parents might need in the future. Finally, one-fourth and one-fifth of healthy hermits and ailing outgoers, respectively, are interested in paying for insurance that would provide their aged parents assistance with money management and bill payment (should they need it), in comparison to slightly more than one-tenth of frail recluses.

CHAPTER 6

Summary and Implications for Marketing Strategy

In order to make the results of the studies presented in the previous two chapters more useful to practitioners, the present chapter highlights the major findings by presenting information in the context of a strategic marketing framework. Specifically, information is presented for select industries or groups of products and services. Implications for market segmentation, product positioning, and marketing mix decisions are recommended for each industry or group category.

The need for designing industry-specific marketing strategies was highlighted by findings of the two studies. Not only were older consumers found to respond differently based on their gerontographic characteristic, but also their responses to marketing strategies varied based on the type of product or service involved. Marketing strategies presented in this chapter apply to the following industry groups:

- food products, food stores, and restaurants
- apparel and footwear
- pharmaceutical products
- housing
- travel and leisure services
- financial services
- high-tech products and related services
- health-care products and services
- insurance services

For each industry-specific product or service category, information is provided in the following areas (to the extent that gerontographic group differences emerged and strategies are relevant to a specific type of product or service).

Market segmentation: major gerontographic-based segments.

Product positioning: major themes likely to appeal to a specific gerontographic segment.

Product: preference for specific types of products or services; preferences for specific product features.

Pricing: price reductions, manufacturer rebates, and preferences for billing/payment methods.

Distribution: preference for distribution methods; preference for direct marketing methods and specific direct marketing considerations.

Promotion: advertising, personal selling, sales promotion, and publicity.

MARKETING STRATEGIES FOR MANUFACTURERS OF FOOD PRODUCTS, FOOD STORES, AND RESTAURANTS

A. Food Products

Viable Segments: *healthy indulgers* and *ailing outgoers.*

1. Healthy Indulgers

Product Positioning: emphasize the product's nutritional value and its aroma.

Marketing Mix Decisions:

• Pricing: frequent use of price reductions or special sales.

• Promotion: stimulate word-of-mouth advertising.

2. Ailing Outgoers

Product Positioning: position food products on taste.

Marketing Mix Decisions:

• Products: develop products that are easy to use, with clear labeling and instructions; develop products that appeal to people with certain physical/ health requirements.

• Pricing: offer rebates.

• Promotion: use coupons in sales promotion; properly stereotype older people in ads, and emphasize group conformity.

• Distribution: allocate funds to educate retail personnel about product benefits.

B. Food Stores

Viable Segment: older consumers in all four groups patronize food stores. However, older consumers differ in the way they respond to marketing factors, with *ailing outgoers* being the group most responsive to various offerings of food stores and supermarkets.

Marketing Mix Decisions:

• Product assortment: carry familiar brands/items and products suitable to the older person's health needs.

- Pricing: use price reductions, offer various payment options (check, credit).
- Promotion: use senior discounts; train sales clerks and make them aware of older consumers' needs.
- Other store policies and strategies: use directional signs to help older consumers locate items; use liberal product-return and refund policy; offer adequate number of check-out registers; offer special-assistance services.
- Location: locate retail facilities near other retail establishments older consumers tend to patronize; create store environments that offer comfort and opportunities for socialization.

C. Restaurants

Viable Segment: although restaurants are likely to be patronized by older consumers in all four gerontographic groups, *ailing outgoers* appear to be the segment most likely to respond to strategies of restaurants.

Positioning: restaurants should be positioned on convenience to appeal to ailing outgoers.

Marketing Mix Decisions:
- Products/items: items should be familiar to older consumers, and suitable to their dietary needs; menus should be made easy to read and locate entries.
- Promotion: use senior discounts; offer special-assistance services, such as package carry-out; create word-of-mouth communication among older customers.
- Other: locate facilities near other places older consumers patronize.

MARKETING STRATEGIES FOR APPAREL AND FOOTWEAR

Viable Segments: viable market segments for apparel and footwear products are *healthy indulgers* and *ailing outgoers*.

1. Healthy Indulgers

Positioning: emphasize social acceptance and approval by same-age peers.

Marketing Mix Decisions: for healthy indulgers, marketing mix decisions should focus on the channel of distribution, both direct marketing and at the retail level.
- Distribution: because healthy indulgers place a great deal of emphasis on product assortment, they do not perceive mail order to be a viable channel (due to limited assortments), preferring to purchase apparel and footwear from retail outlets.

  Department stores should carry well-known brand names of apparel and footwear products; they should offer special-assistance services, and make it easy for the older customer to locate merchanidse.

- Advertising: television and print ads should be used to promote apparel and footwear products to healthy indulgers. Ads should emphasize brand names and group conformity and acceptance.

2. Ailing Outgoers

Ailing outgoers is the segment most likely to respond to the various marketing activities of the apparel and footwear marketer.

Positioning: product positioning for ailing outgoers should focus on two broad domains: product functionality/performance and social acceptance.

Marketing Mix Decisions:

- Product: apparel and footwear products should be of greater appeal to ailing outgoers when they meet their physical needs, such as sizes that fit and special features (e.g., velcro fasteners instead of zippers).
- Pricing: special discount programs such as senior discounts, "sales," rebates, and coupons should induce repeat purchase.
- Advertising: although ailing outgoers are not the group most likely to buy apparel products through mail-order catalogs, they prefer to receive information about new apparel or footwear products in the mail. Informal seminars could also be used for informing ailing outgoers about new fashion products.

    In developing advertising appeals, the emphasis should be on group conformity and social acceptance.

- Distribution: retail outlets, especially department stores distributing apparel and footwear products, should emphasize the following:
  –ease of finding merchandise suitable to one's needs
  –"special" sales
  –special-assistance services (e.g., alterations)
  –wide assortment consisting of well-known brands
  –social acceptance (popular outlets)
  –convenience in doing business

    Direct marketers of apparel and footwear products should emphasize:

  –brand names
  –selection (variety of sizes, styles, features, etc.)
  –prompt delivery
  –free pick-up service for returns

MARKETING STRATEGIES FOR PHARMACEUTICAL PRODUCTS

Viable Segment: *ailing outgoers* are by far the segment that uses most prescription drugs and personal-care products.

Positioning: pharmaceutical products can be positioned on several domains, since ailing outgoers are likely to perceive a variety of reasons as relevant to the purchase and consumption of these products. Some of the underlying themes suggested by our research include:

- ease of product use, including ease of reading information on labels/brochures
- special "deals," such as sales, coupons, and rebates
- social acceptance/approval of those who use the product or brand

Marketing Mix Decisions:

- Product: develop product with easy-to-use features (e.g., packages, information/directions). Ailing outgoers use a variety of pharmaceutical products and demand wide product assortments.
- Pricing: give a variety of price-savings incentives, such as rebates and coupons.
- Promotion: ailing outgoers are receptive to a wide variety of promotional tools.
  - advertisements should properly depict older users of pharmaceutical products
  - some promotional expenditures could be allocated for educating pharmacists and sales representatives of personal-care products
- Distribution: ailing outgoers are responsive to a variety of distribution methods as well as policies of pharmaceutical-product distributors. Drug stores and pharmacies should:
  - carry well-known brands of pharmaceutical products
  - help customers find the products on sale
  - have "specials," such as products on sale and senior discounts
  - make shopping easy and pleasant (e.g., by locating near their prime market segment)
  - train salespeople/pharmacists to be more responsive to the needs of the older customer

     Direct marketers of pharmaceutical and personal-care products should:
  - stress "convenience" in their marketing communications
  - reduce risk by offering reasonable order-cancellation or return policies
  - make an 800 (toll-free) number available to customers
  - provide free pick-up service for returns
  - emphasize prompt product delivery
  - accept several types of credit cards
  - emphasize savings by ordering direct

MARKETING STRATEGIES FOR HOUSING

Our findings suggest four different "sets" of marketing strategies, each focusing on specific types of housing: single-family houses; apartments, townhouses, or condominiums; retirement communities; and nursing homes.

A. Single-Family Houses

Viable Segment: the best market for single-family homes appears to be the *frail recluses*. Older adults in this segment are not only more likely than people in other segments to occupy a single-family house, but also plan to live in such a house (perhaps the same one) in the foreseeable future.

Positioning: single-family homes should be positioned on the basis of their accessibility to medical, personal, and home-care services.

Marketing Mix Decisions: while our research has not provided information on every variable of the marketing mix to suggest specific marketing strategies, it has suggested important factors for builders who wish to appeal to this segment (frail recluses) of the older population. Some key implications:

• locate housing projects near hospitals.

• offer as part of the association fee, or on an "à la carte" basis, several types of personal and home-care services that promote independent living.

• promote accessibility of the housing project to personal, health, and home-care services.

• emphasize personal selling.

B. Apartments, Townhouses, or Condominiums

Viable Segment: *healthy indulgers* appear to be the most viable segment, as it is shown by this group's present preference for apartments, townhouses, or condominiums.

Positioning: these housing projects should be positioned to healthy indulgers on the basis of their locational convenience and security.

Marketing Mix Decisions:

• Developers of apartments, townhouses, or condominiums should build such projects near shopping centers. These structures should include home-security systems and offer access to home-care services either as part of the association fee or on an "à la carte" basis.

• Promotion of these housing projects should emphasize proximity to various types of retail facilities and services, and access to various types of personal and home-care services, as well as security.

• Personal selling should be included in the marketer's promotional mix.

C. Retirement Communities

Viable Segment: *ailing outgoers* appear to be the most viable segment for retirement communities.

Positioning: in order to appeal to the ailing outgoers, marketers should position retirement communities as facilities that promote independence and as viable housing alternatives to increasing costs of maintaining a single-family house.

Marketing Mix Decisions:

- Developers of retirement communities should build such facilities at places that have access to public transportation, personal, and home-care services. They should promote both accessibility to such services as well as personal and home security.

- Ailing outgoers find seminars as very useful ways of getting information about various housing options.

D. Nursing Homes

Viable Segments: the two most viable market segments for nursing homes are *ailing outgoers* and *healthy indulgers*.

1. Ailing Outgoers

There appears to be no rationale for developing a different strategy for marketing nursing homes to ailing outgoers. This group does not seem to value any of the attributes examined in this study more than other gerontographic groups.

2. Healthy Indulgers

Positioning: in order to appeal to healthy indulgers, nursing homes should position themselves as facilities that provide continuous health-care assistance as an alternative to a hospital.

Marketing Mix Decisions:

- In designing nursing homes and amenities to appeal to healthy indulgers, nursing homes should focus on the availability of (accessibility to) health-care services and to a lesser extent upon the provision of planned social activities.

- The marketer's promotional mix should emphasize personal selling.

MARKETING STRATEGIES FOR TRAVEL AND LEISURE SERVICES

A. Airlines/Cruise Lines

Viable Segment: *healthy indulgers.*

Positioning: emphasizes convenience and price.

Marketing Mix Decisions:

- Product: offer a wide range of travel-related services.

- Pricing: offer special prices to groups through membership programs.

• Promotion: offer senior discounts; properly stereotype older people in ads; use testimonials.

• Distribution: emphasize the ease of obtaining travel-related services by phone or by mail.

B. Hotels/Motels

Primary Segment: *ailing outgoers.*

Positioning: position hotels on "value."

Marketing Mix Decisions:

• Product: develop alliances with other providers of travel/leisure services to provide a wider "package" or assortment of services.

• Pricing: offer special group-membership deals; use fast check-approval policies.

• Promotion: offer senior discounts; use proper age stereotyping in ads; train staff to assist customers with various forms; and set up free seminars to promote services.

• Distribution: develop clientele mailing list and train representatives to effectively deal with customers over the phone.

MARKETING STRATEGIES FOR FINANCIAL SERVICES

Although older adults in different gerontographic groups have different preferences for financial services, they are not necessarily equally viable for the various types of financial-service providers. Thus, a group may prefer to receive certain types of financial services but only from a selected group of financial-service providers. Thus, the findings suggest not only general implications for financial-service providers but also institution-specific marketing strategies—that is, the types of services on which various institutions should focus when trying to reach older customers in the four groups.

A. General Marketing Strategies for Financial Institutions

Primary Segment: *healthy indulgers* appear to be the group most likely to demand a variety of financial services.

Positioning: financial services should be positioned for healthy indulgers on the basis of convenience and personal relationship; long-term investments should be positioned as vehicles that would enable them to pay for post-retirement expenses, such as home improvements.

Marketing Mix Decisions:

• Products/Services (see also "institution-specific")

–financial advice (for a fee)
–overdraft privilege or personal line of credit
–free financial services for keeping large balances
–moderate- and low-risk investments

• Distribution

–personal visit (e.g., private banking)
–maintain efficient telemarketing system

• Promotion

–telemarketing
–train personnel/staff to assist customers with a variety of questions
–emphasize locational convenience in ads

Secondary Segment: *frail recluses* appear to be the next best market for financial services.

Positioning: investment products such as IRAs/Keoghs and home-equity loans should be positioned as vehicles that would enable frail recluses to pay for a variety of expenses they are likely to have in later life, including improvements to their existing homes and long-term care.

Marketing Mix Decisions:

• Products (see also "institution-specific")

–overdraft privilege or personal line of credit
–IRA/Keogh accounts
–reverse mortgage plan: preference for receiving all cash now and making cash payments to lender

• Distribution:

–personnel should be available in various branches that would provide assistance with filling out forms.

• Promotion:

–sales representatives need to spend extra time explaining various financial services
–use senior discounts

B. Viable Segments for Specific Types of Financial Institutions

1. Viable Segments for Specific Services Marketed by Commercial Banks

Financial planning: healthy indulgers and frail recluses

Money market funds: ailing outgoers and frail recluses

Stocks: ailing outgoers and frail recluses

Tax advice: ailing outgoers and frail recluses

Insurance policies: ailing outgoers and frail recluses

Savings/checking accounts: frail recluses

Certificates of deposit (CDs): frail recluses

Government bonds/U.S. T-bills: frail recluses

Asset-management services: frail recluses

2. *Viable Segments for Specific Services Marketed by Credit Unions*

Financial planning: ailing outgoers and frail recluses

Savings/checking accounts: healthy indulgers and frail recluses

Certificates of deposit (CDs): frail recluses

IRA/Keogh: frail recluses

Tax advice: frail recluses

Insurance policies: frail recluses

3. *Viable Segments for Specific Services Marketed by S&Ls*

Financial planning: ailing outgoers and frail recluses

Money market funds: frail recluses

Certificates of deposit (CDs): healthy indulgers

Government bonds/U.S. T-bills: ailing outgoers and frail recluses

Stocks: healthy indulgers

IRA/Keogh: frail recluses

Insurance policies: frail recluses

4. *Viable Segments for Specific Services Marketed by Stock Brokerage Companies*

Money market funds: healthy hermits

Savings/checking accounts: ailing outgoers

Government bonds/U.S. T-bills: healthy hermits

IRA Keogh: healthy hermits, ailing outgoers, and healthy indulgers

Certificates of deposit (CDs): ailing outgoers

Stocks: healthy indulgers and healthy hermits

Tax advice: healthy hermits, healthy indulgers, and ailing outgoers

Insurance policies: healthy hermits

Asset-management services: healthy hermits

5. *Viable Segments for Specific Services Marketed by AARP*

Money market funds: frail recluses

Government bonds/U.S. T-bills: healthy indulgers, ailing outgoers, and frail recluses

Certificates of deposit (CDs): frail recluses

Financial planning: ailing outgoers

Savings/checking accounts: ailing outgoers

Tax advice: healthy indulgers, ailing outgoers, and frail recluses

IRA/Keogh: frail recluses

6. *Viable Segments for Specific Financial Services Marketed by Mutual Fund Companies*

Money market funds: healthy hermits

Stocks: healthy hermits

IRA/Keogh: healthy hermits and healthy indulgers

Government bonds/U.S. T-bills: healthy indulgers and frail recluses

Asset-management services: healthy indulgers

MARKETING STRATEGIES FOR HIGH-TECH PRODUCTS AND SERVICES

Viable Segments: primary segments vary according to the type of product or service.

- Home-security systems: frail recluses and healthy indulgers
- Telephone-answering machine: healthy indulgers
- Energy-saving appliances or installed devices: frail recluses and healthy indulgers
- Automobiles: healthy indulgers
- Operated-assisted services: ailing outgoers, healthy indulgers, and frail recluses
- Discount "package" long-distance telephone plans: ailing outgoers, healthy indulgers, and frail recluses

Strategies by Segment:

Healthy Indulgers and Ailing Outgoers:

- promote new products and services through organized groups; present information in group settings
- emphasize convenience in buying direct

Frail Recluses:

- advertise on print and TV media

- use personal selling
- use senior member discounts
- accept personal checks
- when marketing electronic products direct, emphasize acceptance of a variety of credit cards and availability of a toll-free number

Healthy Hermits:
- emphasize/offer free-pick-up service for returns (for electronic products sold through the mail or stores)

Ailing Outgoers:
- offer/emphasize senior or member discounts

MARKETING STRATEGIES FOR HEALTH-CARE PRODUCTS AND SERVICES

Viable Segments: since health-care products and services vary widely (e.g., preventive, acute, and long-term care), specific types of products and services are of appeal to different gerontographic segments, even though ailing outgoers appear to be the group most likely to be the heaviest users of such products and services in general. Thus, strategies are suggested separately for the most viable groups.

Viable Segments for Specific Products/Services:
- Exercise equipment: frail recluses
- Prescription drugs: ailing outgoers
- Dietary meals: ailing outgoers
- Self-diagnostics: frail recluses
- Health club memberships: ailing outgoers and healthy indulgers
- Paid at-home assistance: healthy indulgers
- Health membership programs: frail recluses and ailing outgoers
- Home-health care: frail recluses

Positioning:

Healthy Indulgers: position services provided by health-care professionals and hospitals on "reputation"

Ailing Outgoers: position services provided by hospitals and health-care professionals on "reasonable prices/fees"

Frail Recluses: position health-care service providers and hospitals on "convenience"

Marketing Mix Decisions:

• Promotion:

Healthy Indulgers: use TV or print ads; use testimonials

Ailing Outgoers: use direct mail and telephone/personal contacts; use senior discounts and membership programs; avoid age-stereotyping in ads

Frail Recluses: use direct mail and group membership programs; properly stereotype recipients of health-care services in ads

• Pricing:

Healthy Indulgers: this group is not price sensitive; price according to the value of services

Ailing Outgoers: prices should be reasonable

Frail Recluses: make available several methods of payment for services

• Distribution:

Healthy Indulgers: offer "packages" of preventive health-care services

Ailing Outgoers: enhance direct contact systems for appointments, feedback, and health-monitoring services

Frail Recluses: offer locational convenience (e.g., health clinics, accessibility to hospitals)

MARKETING STRATEGIES FOR INSURANCE SERVICES

Viable Segments: three gerontographic groups (healthy indulgers, ailing outgoers, and frail recluses) are viable segments for a variety of insurance products.

• Long-term care: healthy indulgers, ailing outgoers, and frail recluses
• "Medigap": ailing outgoers
• Car insurance: healthy indulgers
• Home-health care: ailing outgoers

Positioning: positioning appears to be viable only for *ailing outgoers*, since this group is most sensitive to various offerings of the insurance-service providers. "Convenience" is one broad dimension on which insurance providers can position their services.

Marketing Mix Decisions for Marketing to Ailing Outgoers:

• Promotion:

–sponsor events where there is an opportunity to explain new products to groups of older adults
–use senior discounts

–offer incentives to sales force for cross-selling related products

–use incentives to present customers and firms selling related products (e.g., investments) to recommend the company's products to prospective customers

• Pricing:

–offer competitive premiums for comparable policies

–offer a variety of payment systems/plans

–give special discounts to those who belong to certain groups (e.g., AARP) or are members of special promotional programs

• Distribution:

–consider developing partnerships with nontraditional service providers, such as banks and AARP

–develop efficient and effective telemarketing

–emphasize convenience of buying direct

• Products:

–develop wide product assortments of insurance and investment products

–provide assistance with filling out forms as a complementary service

–offer liberal cancellation and refund policies

–make policy coverage effective as quickly as possible

–in developing long-term care policies, include the following benefits:

  home care and personal care

  companion or monitoring services

  nutrition and preventive health-care programs

  legal and tax advice

  adult day care

  transportation and escort services

  money management and bill payment

CHAPTER 7

Potential Applications and Usefulness

The Life-Stage model presented has a wide range of potential applications to the field of marketing. These vary from database marketing to identifying potential customers and developing specific marketing strategies. This chapter discusses such applications and elaborates on the usefulness of the model. In order to demonstrate the model's usefulness, we use existing databases, both academic and commercial, to show how the gerontographic segments can be linked to these existing resources to enhance their value and vice versa. Specifically, we demonstrate four potential applications of the Life-Stage model: (1) linking gerontographic segments to other (existing) databases; (2) linking each of the segments to specific products and services; (3) identifying present and prospective customers; and (4) developing marketing strategies.

LINKING LIFE STAGES TO OTHER DATABASES

Marketers can use the Life-Stage model to enrich the value of their databases when they conduct market studies. Organizations targeting healthy hermits, ailing outgoers, frail recluses, and healthy indulgers can add information on mass media, product purchase, and zip code specific to each segment, for example, to infer the segment's media-use habits, buying patterns, credit use, geographic location, and the like. Each gerontographic segment could then be profiled in greater detail. For example, marketers may seek answers to questions such as: What media does a specific segment use? What types of products and brands does each segment buy on a frequent basis? What type(s) of outlets do they prefer? We have already given several examples of similar variables that are linked to marketing strategy based on our surveys. Such information should be of greater value to marketers than information found in existing databases because it is product- and segment-specific and can be translated into marketing strategy.

Second, data from other lifestyle models such as VALS also can be linked to the gerontographic segments to enhance the value of these existing databases and help develop behaviorally sensitive marketing strategies. For example, a marketer targeting a market segment in SRI's LAVOA model (see description in Chapter 3) can determine the specific gerontographic group that dominates it and design appropriate marketing strategies for his or her products, promotion, pricing, and distribution. In order to be able to link the two databases, one can use either a direct or an indirect method. The first method involves obtaining information necessary in constructing both models (e.g., lifestyles, media use, demographics) and then determining the segments in the one model that contain the proportionately largest number of individuals classified by the criteria used in the second model. The indirect method involves the use of variables common in both models. For example, once the marketer identifies the types of products or media used by a segment in one model, one can look for segments in the other model that make heavy use of the same types of products or media.

Both methods of linking the Life-Stage model to other models have advantages and disadvantages. With the direct method, one can obtain more recent and accurate information from the marketplace, but the amount of information one can gather would be limited, since large amounts of information can be expensive or may result in less accurate information due to respondent fatigue. On the other hand, the indirect method can be less expensive and provides access to larger amounts of information available in other databases, but the accuracy and recency of information is sacrificed. Furthermore, one must decide on the most appropriate variables that would provide the most effective link between the two databases. Intersegment sensitivity to the criteria used (e.g., media, products) should be high; that is, one cannot use variables that show intersegment variation in one model but not in the other. Thus, variables with the highest intersegment sensitivity should be used. Similarly, variables which are present in more than one segment of the models (databases) should be avoided. The focus should be on identifying those characteristics and consumption-related behaviors (such as product use and media use) which are *predominately* descriptive of each one of the four segments.

By linking the Life-Stage model to other commercial databases, one can obtain a wealth of information presently available in existing commercial databases. Such information is product/service-specific (e.g., brand purchased, dollar amount spent). Similarly, the value of existing databases can be enhanced considerably because these commercial sources do not contain information on older consumers' sensitivity to marketing strategies. Thus, for example, a marketer of financial services interested in reaching older adults who are heavy users of low-risk investments could learn about the specific gerontographic segment(s) which are are most receptive to these investments, as well as the types of marketing strategies that would be most effective in reaching each desirable segment.

LINKING LIFE STAGES TO PRODUCTS AND SERVICES

How can a marketer determine the life-stage segment(s) is (are) most viable for specific products and services? Two main approaches can be used: first, one can use primary data from the marketplace in the form of surveys; and second, secondary data can be used to infer the viability of a given gerontographic segment (based on published or previously gathered data). In the following sections, we will explain how the two methods can be used, as well as their advantages and disadvantages; and we will present examples to illustrate how one can make use of each method of linking our life-stage groups to specific products or services.

Primary Data

Use of primary data to link life-stage groups to specific products or services is considered to be the most direct and accurate method. This approach requires the analyst to take three steps: (1) gather relevant information, (2) analyze the information gathered to construct the life-stage segments, and (3) assess each segment's sensitivity to specific marketing stimuli for a given product or service.

Gathering information from the marketplace is a relatively easy task. Information can be gathered by means of various survey instruments, through interviews or mail surveys; it could also involve gathering information from more "controlled" studies such as field experiments. Regardless of the method of data gathering, the market analyst must gather three types of information: (1) information necessary for constructing the gerontographic segments or life-stage groups; (2) data on consumer use of, or preferences for, specific products and services; and (3) information on older consumers' responses to specific marketing strategies commonly used (as well as emerging strategies) in marketing specific products or services.

The information needed to construct the life-stage groups must be based on relevant theory and research on older consumers' behavior in later life. Knowledge of the forces that affect behavior in later life and their implications for consumer behavior are crucial in specifying key variables to be included in the Life-Stage model. Supportive research studies can also be used to validate the need for considering a theoretical framework and specific variables derived from such a framework. Although we are tempted to recommend specific frameworks or types of variables that should be used for constructing the four life-stage segments, the dynamic forces that shape the marketplace (e.g., consumers, marketers, product offerings) and our evolving knowledge about older consumers dictate the use of variables that take these changes into consideration. We have provided, however, a framework (Chapter 3) consisting of relevant theories that suggest the use of specific types of variables. Such variables include (but are not limited to) psychological variables such as attitudes, personality, lifestyles,

self-perception, needs and role perceptions; social variables such as social roles
and life-cycle changes; and selected life events, physical and sociodemographic
variables that "locate" the person in his or her social environment or affect his/
her psychological and physical well-being. These variables must be revisited
periodically to update the list so that relevant variables are always included.
(This need is reflected in the revisions of other commercial general segmentation
models such as VALS, which has been revised to VALS2 to reflect social trends
and changes.) For example, the availability of long-term care insurance, increasing numbers of social service agencies, and corporate support of their employees
who are caregivers to their older relatives, coupled with the increasing number
of women in the labor force, may have affected the older person's attitudes,
needs, and role perceptions regarding care-giving and care-receiving, and
therefore one's transition into a specific life stage. Such attitudes, needs, and
role perceptions should be included in the list of variables used to construct the
Life-Stage model, to the extent they affect consumer behavior.

The second type of information a market analyst must gather is information
on product/service use or preference. This information should be product- or
service-specific, since we have demonstrated the value of such industry-specific
information. Specific product/service-use information can be in the form of use
of specific brands or service-provider patronage behavior; and it can include
other behavioral variables. Variables which are used by mailing list companies,
such as products purchased and magazine readership habits, should be given the
highest priority because once a segment's profile is developed on the basis of
such factors, the desirable group could be easily reached through direct mail.
Preference for specific products/services, brands, or service providers can be
collected in the form of attitudinal data. When new products or services are
involved, information on interest or purchase likelihood is more relevant, provided that the researcher can accurately describe the new product or service to
potential users.

Finally, the market analyst must gather information on older consumer responses to specific marketing strategies, tactics, or marketing stimuli. These
would be variables a marketer contemplates using as part of his/her marketing
mix, such as use of senior discounts, older spokespersons in ads, special services
that appeal to older adults (e.g., valet parking, package wrapping), and the like.
The analyst should obtain such information in surveys by asking respondents to
indicate if the particular marketing stimulus makes a difference (i.e., is important) in their decision to choose a product, brand, vendor, etc.

Once the primary data are collected, the analyst must develop the life-stage
segments. This procedure was described earlier (Chapter 3). As new variables
might have to be considered, the analyst should examine the relevance of such
variables by correlating them to certain consumer behaviors, such as product or
service use and responses to other marketing stimuli. The stronger the correlations, or the larger the number of marketing-related stimuli these variables cor-

relate with, the more suitable they should be for their inclusion in the set of variables to be used in constructing the Life-Stage model.

The last stage in using primary data to link the life-stage groups to specific products or services, and to validate the assumption that users of such products and services should be treated differently in the development of marketing strategies, involves presentation of rationale for target marketing. In order to accomplish this task, the analyst must first assess how each market segment (life-stage group) behaves with respect to various types of products or services. This can be done by cross-classifying product/service use and preferences by each of the four groups. The larger the differences among the groups, the stronger the justification for target marketing. By performing a similar analysis on each variable of the marketing mix that a marketer considers implementing, one can determine the extent to which differentiated or undifferentiated marketing strategy can be justified for reaching one or more market segments, as well as the extent to which specific marketing strategies and tactics should be used in targeting a given life-stage segment.

Secondary Data

The life-stage groups can also be linked to specific products or services by means of available data (published or previously collected). In order to do this, the analyst must know (1) how the use of certain products (one may or may not be interested in) correlates with the use of products one is primarily interested in, and (2) how the former type of products relates to the life-stage segments. The assumption made here is that if preference for a product not related to the marketer's interest correlates with the use of a product one is interested in, and the product of no interest is preferred by a given life-stage segment, then products of interest to the analyst should also be preferred by the same segment.

This assumption is based on the rather well-established fact that people do not purchase products and services on a random basis; rather, the purchase and consumption of products and services in general are systematically related based on one's needs, income, lifestyles, and other characteristics. For example, an event such as birth of a child creates the need for a variety of products and services such as baby foods, clothing, toys, and health-care services. This assumption does not need to be tested; rather, the issue is: How many of these products and services (the breadth or variety of products and services) are related, and how are they related? Thus, if one product is demanded by a life-stage segment, the same segment should also demand another product which relates to the one in demand.

It is rather easy for the research analyst to examine and establish patterns of consumption among various types of products and services by reviewing published studies that show relationships among products and services. Published studies in one's field often show relationships among products/services in the form of correlations, cross-classifications, or as an output of more sophisticated statistical analyses such as factor analysis and multidimensional scaling. In order to illustrate one such source, we are presenting the results of factor analysis of products and services that older respondents in one of our studies indicated they use or would like to use (Table 7.1).

Table 7.1 shows groupings of products and services into categories. These groupings were determined by mathematically examining patterns of respondent preferences across the products and services. Those products or services which older consumers prefer as a group are separated from others, and are grouped together because they have something in common—perhaps an underlying need for their use, a function they perform for the older person, or because they are part of certain lifestyles. We have "labeled" these groups based on these latent meanings or needs these products satisfy. For illustration purposes, the importance lies upon the relationships among products rather than upon the correctness of the labels used. Thus, for example, if one product or service is desirable to a life-stage segment, chances are that other products and services from the same group will be preferred by the same segment as well.

IDENTIFYING PRESENT AND PROSPECTIVE CUSTOMERS

Another potential use of the Life-Stage model for marketers is in identifying present and prospective customers for specific products and services. By examining product preferences across life-stage segments, marketers can determine whether the primary market for a given product or service presently is the healthy hermits, ailing outgoers, frail recluses, or healthy indulgers. By identifying selected characteristics that define or exclusively describe each of these groups, marketers can obtain mailing lists and phone numbers for direct marketing; or they can examine the specific group's inclination to respond to other marketing activities of the firm for developing target-marketing strategies.

Because people in various gerontographic segments are classified based on information pertaining to various aging processes, events, and circumstances in later life, a prospective customer's classification or transition into a given life stage (and his/her subsequent development of needs for specific products and services as a result of such a transition) can be predicted with event-history-analysis (or hazard) models. Thus, individuals who are "at risk" of moving into a given life stage can be identified and profiled, enabling the marketer to be proactive in targeting older adults who are anticipating life-stage changes and, as a result, are in the process of developing needs for new types of products and services. This can be done by examining the variables that carry the heaviest weight in predicting one's transition into the next stage (see Appendix A), where such a transition can be modeled as an event (see "Theoretical Foundations for the Life-Stage Model"). This approach would give the marketer an edge over competition because one can proactively position a product or service when the need for it is about to develop among a group of prospective buyers.

Table 7.1
Product/Service-Use Groupings Based on Factor Analysis

Special-needs products/services
 Dietary program or dietary meal prescription
 Self-diagnostic medical equipment (at home)
 TV channel having only talk shows about topics like "health," "shopping,"
   "finances," "medicine," and "housing"
 Books/videocassettes for people at your stage in life, helping them deal with a
   variety of matters that concern them

Self-Improvement/cultural
 "Learning how to" cassette tapes or books
 Arts, crafts, music, or other adult education classes
 Season tickets to theater, ballet, concert, or ball games

Technology-based products/services
 Videocassette recorder (VCR)
 Microwave oven
 Cordless phone
 Custom telephone services (like "call waiting")
 Premium cable TV channels (like HBO, Cinemax)

Independent-living enhancement products/services
 Medical-care services provided at your home
 Home-care services (like cleaning, grass mowing, etc.)
 Home in a planned retirement community (for personal use)

Personal appearance/convenience
 Hair-care or face-care products
 Latest style of clothes
 Fast-food delivery services (food delivered to your home)

Health/wealth preservation
 Health club membership
 Whole life insurance (you pay for protection and savings)
 Special travel membership or discount card (like hotel, airline, car rental)

Investment instruments
 Money market account
 Stocks and bonds or mutual funds

Home-enhancement products
 Smoke or fire detector
 "Do-it-yourself" hobbies (like woodworking, knitting, etc.)
 Burglar alarm system

Banking services
 Automatic deposit of your check (EFT)
 Automated bank-teller machines (ATMs)

Life-stage specific
 Membership to associations serving people over a certain age
 Health insurance
 Energy-saving appliances or installed devices
 Townhouse, condominium, or apartment (negative correlation)

DEVELOPING MARKETING STRATEGY

Finally, the Life-Stage model can be used by marketers in developing marketing strategy. Because the link between a specific life-stage segment and that segment's responses to marketing stimuli (tactics and strategies) has been established—that is, we have demonstrated that each of the four segments responds differently to various types of marketing efforts—one can see the usefulness of using these segment-specific responses in developing marketing strategies and programs for the mature market. Furthermore, we have demonstrated that older consumers' responses to such marketing efforts vary by type of product or service, suggesting the value of the Life-Stage model in formulating product/service- or industry-specific marketing strategies. Finally, the data from our two national studies have shown that product-specific strategies may be more appealing to certain life-stage segments, suggesting the need for targeting each segment with different marketing strategies and marketing programs for specific types of consumer products and services.

The Life-Stage model presented helps marketers refine and fine-tune their marketing strategies in several additional ways. For example, with respect to mass-media strategy development, each of the four life-stage segments shows preferences for different types of mass media; and even when specific media are preferred by a particular segment, chances are that not all media vehicles are likely to have the same effectiveness. For example, while *Modern Maturity* is one of the most frequently read magazine, it is more likely to reach the healthy hermits than any of the remaining three gerontographic groups. Similarly, *TV Guide* is most likely to be read by ailing outgoers, *Newsweek* by healthy indulgers, while food and cooking types of magazines appeal primarily to frail recluses.

When combined with other databases, the Life-Stage model can yield additional useful information for strategy development. In much the same way other psychographic models (e.g., VALS) have been linked to different databases (e.g., PRISM) by means of information contained in the two databases (e.g., zip codes), the same methods can be used to integrate the four life-stage segments with existing commercial databases. For example, zip codes can be used for geo-coding. Since we have presented data showing higher concentrations of gerontographic groups in certain geographic regions, there is a greater likelihood that geographic differences will be more noticeable in more narrowly defined geographic areas such as states, counties, or specific regions defined by zip codes. Rather than arbitrarily defining geographic regions, the analyst who wishes to determine the gerontographic (or life-stage) profile of a given region could first define such regions based on similarities of older adults with respect to available demographic characteristics (e.g., education, income, living arrangements, housing type) available in large geo-demographic databases such as PRISM, Sales Management, and Census. Zip codes listed under each geographic region would then be matched with zip codes listed under each life-stage segment obtained from responses of survey participants. In doing so, the geronto-graphic profile of a specific geographic location can be determined and, based on such a profile and product or service marketed, specific marketing strategy could be effectively developed for specific regions.

Additional criteria can be used to link the Life-Stage model to other commercial databases. For example, we have shown that preferences for various products, services, and mass media vary across gerontographic groups, and that there are systematic patterns (relationships) among such preferences. Therefore, databases that contain very detailed information on product preferences and mass media habits (e.g., Mediamark Research, Inc. reports) could be particularly useful in identifying products, services, and media preferred by each of the life-stage groups. This can be accomplished by correlating variables showing consumption of specific products and services, mass media preferences, and the like to form ''clusters'' or groupings of such products (and services) older consumers tend to use. Preferences for products and services revealed in surveys could then be matched to broader groupings (based on larger databases) which contain various types of consumption information. Thus, once the marketer decides on the specific product or service to be marketed, and on databases that contain information on life-stage groups, one could determine the effective strategy for marketing—from market segmentation and targeting to specific marketing programs and tactics that would produce the most effective response.

Definitions, Measures, and Explanations of Aging

TYPES AND DEFINITIONS OF AGING

TYPES AND DEFINITIONS OF AGING	MEASURES	EXPLANATIONS OF AGING — Perspectives	Brief Description
Biological (also known as physiological, functional)—changes in cells and tissues resulting in the physical deterioration of the biological system and its susceptibility to disease and mortality.	Physical condition of the main bodily systems (e.g., cardiovascular, musculoskel-etal) weighted differently in the biological age equation.	Programming theories	Aging is intrinsic, genetic, and developmental; natural and expected result written into the genes.
		Error (stochastic, environmental) theories	Aging depends on accumulation of environmental insults, causing damage to the body cells, resulting in malfunction of cells, molecules, and organs over time.
Psychological—development and changes in:		Organismic approach	Humans are active constructors of knowledge; development occurs intrinsically in stages of cognitive structure.
(a) cognition—i.e., the process of perception, memory, judgment, reasoning, and decision making (often known as "human development"); and	Capability to perform cognitive tasks assessed by tests such as Wechsler Adult Intelligence Scale.	Mechanistic approach	Humans are reactive; knowledge reflects the external environment.
		Contextual approach	Development is the result of reciprocal and bidirectional process between individual and environment.
(b) personality and self—i.e., how others see you with respect to your attitudes and behaviors; and how one sees himself, ideal self, and the fit between the two.	Personality traits or dimensions and typologies; self-perception, such as measures of cognitive age.	Psychometric approach	Atheoretical, quantitative approach aimed at uncovering various aspects of cognition over the life span.
Social—changing composite of social relationships, lifestyles, attributes and attitudes, and assumption of social roles people are expected to play at various stages of life (e.g., "father," "retiree," "grandparent").	Closeness of one's values, attitudes, and behaviors to age- or group-related norms associated with various roles; role relationships and social status within a system.	Structural functionalism	Individuals become part of the social order, and their behaviors are reflective of needs and norms of the system.
		Symbolic interactionism	Individuals develop a sense of self by interpreting others' responses to their behavior.
		Exchange	Social interaction is the result of costs and benefits derived from such interactions.
		Marxism	Social distribution of power and resources is embedded within the context of the social relations of production.
		Social phenomenology	Meanings of social roles are constructed within the varied worlds of elderly's experience.

APPENDIX B

Profiles of Life-Stage Groups

The following pages were assembled from recent survey results (or more detailed data in other reports) to describe and profile the four gerontographic groups in the Life-Stage model. Individuals in each segment can be described on the basis of several characteristics, including demographics, consumption-related needs, and how they respond to companies' marketing efforts. These characteristics were not used to form the four segments, but are useful in describing the segments and their consumer behavior. We will use only a small number of such characteristics from two of our surveys to illustrate the heterogeneity of the derived segments. Table B.1 shows demographic characteristics of gerontographic groups; Table B.2 shows consumption-related needs and concerns of older Americans classified into four gerontographic groups; and Table B.3 provides information about their behavior in the marketplace based on responses given to questions in a general (nonindustry specific) national survey. Percentage differences of approximately ±7% between two segments indicate a significant difference ($p < 0.05$ level).

HEALTHY HERMITS

Demographics

Age. Healthy hermits are somewhat older than the average older person over the age of 55. A little over half of them (51.67%) are age 65 and older, the second oldest group after ailing outgoers. Four in ten of the healthy hermits are between the ages of 65 and 75.

Sex. Although six in ten people age 55 and over are female, the female gender is somewhat underrepresented among healthy hermits. About 58% of the older adults in this group are female, which is the second group with the fewest females after ailing outgoers.

Living Arrangements. Healthy hermits are relatively more isolated than older individuals in other gerontographic groups. Seventy-six percent of them live with others, family or nonfamily members, a figure which is the lowest among all four groups.

Education. Older adults in the "healthy hermits" group are rather well-educated. One

Table B.1
Characteristics of Life-Stage Groups

	Healthy Hermits %	Ailing Outgoers %	Frail Recluses %	Healthy Indulgers %
Age: 55-64	48.32	55.03	46.32	54.53
65-74	40.39	36.18	42.50	36.49
75+	11.28	8.79	11.18	8.97
Sex: Female (%)	57.97	62.50	54.38	64.84
Living Arrangement: Living with others (%)	76.02	77.38	80.18	82.24
Marital Status: Married (%)	75.78	74.33	81.41	83.91
Education: College graduate or more (%)	33.12	21.48	24.72	35.11
Retired (%)	58.77	36.19	70.55	30.71
Income: $40,000 or more (%)	37.55	21.38	28.31	37.31
Geographic Location: East	18.12	17.45	10.49	19.70
Northcentral	37.65	36.84	43.59	33.35
South	26.91	29.63	30.64	26.37
West	17.32	16.28	15.28	20.58
Urbanity: Urban %	77.77	79.98	78.96	76.03
TV Viewing: Heavy% (3.5 hours or more daily)	43.25	50.47	57.82	34.38
Radio Listening: Heavy% (2 hours or more daily)	38.31	45.41	38.41	39.29
Newspaper Reading: Heavy % (1.15 hours or more daily)	27.84	27.74	30.27	23.05
Magazine Reading: Heavy % (1 hour or more daily)	52.35	57.63	54.23	53.12

in three has a college education, a figure unusually high for the older population, and slightly lower than that of the "healthy indulgers" group.

Marital Status. Healthy hermits are about as likely as healthy indulgers to be married. These two groups have the lowest number of married older adults, with approximately three-fourths of older adults in these two groups reporting they are married.

Retirement. One of the distinct characteristics of this gerontographic group is the high proportion of older adults who, in relation to their counterparts in some other geronto-

Table B.2
Consumer Behavior of Older Americans by Gerontographic Clusters
(% "Strongly/Somewhat Agree")

	Healthy Hermits	Ailing Outgoers	Frail Recluses	Healthy Indulgers
Money				
Being able to keep up with bills and weekly expenses.	7.34	55.56	31.45	32.18
Being financially independent.	17.78	73.51	43.41	64.55
Health/Well-Being				
Being able to contact someone in case of emergency.	4.72	52.81	29.07	33.50
Being mugged, raped, or robbed.	24.30	56.22	49.71	31.49
Social/Family				
Having to take care of your aging parents.	4.97	21.73	8.50	13.91
Feeling that no one cares for you.	24.30	33.93	24.40	18.79
Home				
Having your home/apartment burned or burglarized.	24.65	61.27	48.65	30.45
Finding someone to do home or applicance repairs.	15.13	32.04	24.74	17.95
Information				
Getting useful information on things that affect you.	16.72	54.52	37.43	60.23
Getting good financial, tax, or legal advice.	20.31	48.46	35.46	46.25
Leisure				
Finding ways to enjoy yourself (like travel and entertainment).	3.53	38.62	3.49	43.01
Being able to attend special events or activities.	2.58	22.83	4.02	14.42
Daily Activities				
Being able to do your shopping and run errands.	7.11	51.62	25.06	33.31
Being able to fix your meals.	1.7	41.48	18.35	25.76

graphic groups, report they are retired. Although this figure is considerably lower than that of the frail recluses, it is much higher than the percentage of retirees in the remaining gerontographic groups.

Income. Healthy hermits along with healthy indulgers have the highest income among all gerontographic groups. Specifically, 37% of all healthy hermits report annual incomes in excess of $40,000, a figure almost twice as high as that of ailing outgoers.

Geographic location. With respect to geographic distribution, healthy hermits are equally distributed throughout the four geographic regions. No region appears to have a higher representation of healthy hermits in relation to other gerontographic groups. The same appears to be the case with respect to urban versus rural location, where healthy

Table B.3
Consumption-Related Needs by Gerontographic Clusters
(% "Very/Somewhat Concerned")

	Healthy Hermits	Ailing Outgoers	Frail Recluses	Healthy Indulgers
Responses to Age-Based Strategies				
Companies should offer more discounts to older than to younger adults.	40.3	65.9	61.5	50.4
I like advertisements that show products especially for older people.	17.8	36.7	25.7	26.8
Responses to Promotional Strategies				
I am attracted to special displays in a store.	29.3	38.9	32.4	42.5
I usually watch the advertisement for announcement of sales.	72.9	79.7	69.6	70.1
New Products				
I like to try something new every time I am in the store.	11.8	16.4	8.8	15.0
I try to learn as much as I can about a new product/service before buying or using it.	76.2	81.0	68.9	77.2
Dis/satisfaction With Products/Services				
I sometimes wish I could get my money back for something I bought.	66.0	82.6	77.7	83.5
I often find packages and containers difficult to open.	60.5	67.2	73.0	63.0
High Tech Products				
Using calculators, computers, and other electronic gadgets is usually too confusing to bother with.	21.1	31.5	36.5	36.2
Older people should learn to use electronic gadgets and services that can make their life easier.	66.7	76.8	65.5	77.9
Payment Systems				
I like to pay cash for most things I buy.	74.2	85.8	78.4	69.3
I seldom pay off the entire balance on my monthly statements of my charge accounts.	9.0	21.2	14.9	18.1

hermits are as likely to live in urban or rural area as older adults in other gerontographic groups.

Mass Media Use. Healthy hermits are not particularly heavy users of mass media. When compared to other gerontographic groups, they do not show they use significantly more or less of the various media—television, radio, newspapers, and magazines.

Needs

Money. Healthy hermits is the group least concerned with keeping up with bills and weekly expenses, with only a small percentage of them (7.34%) expressing concern. The older adults in this life-stage group are also the least concerned with their ability to be financially independent, with 17.78% expressing such a concern.

Health/Well-Being. Healthy hermits is the gerontographic group least likely to be concerned with their safety and security. Only a small percent (4.72%) indicated concern with getting hold of someone in case of emergency, and only one in four (24.3%) expressed concern with crime (being mugged, raped, or robbed).

Social/Family. Only one in twenty (4.97%) of healthy hermits, the lowest number of any group, expressed concerned with care-giving responsibilities toward their parents. This group as well as healthy indulgers are the least likely to report the feeling that no one cares for them.

Home. Concerns with home-related matters are also the lowest among healthy hermits. One in four (24.65%), almost as many as healthy indulgers, expressed concern with fire and burglary of their home. These two groups are also the least concerned with finding someone to do home or appliance repairs, with 15.13% of healthy hermits expressing concern.

Information. Healthy hermits are by far the gerontographic group least likely to consume information about day-to-day events and activities. Sixteen percent of older adults in this life-stage segment expressed concern with getting useful information on topics that affect them, and only one in five were concerned with getting good financial, tax, or legal advice.

Leisure. The desire for self-indulgence among this group is almost similar to that of frail recluses. The percentage who indicated concern with finding ways to enjoy themselves was almost nil (3.53%). Similarly, only a very small percentage of healthy hermits (2.58%) indicated concern with their ability or inability to attend special events and activities.

Daily Activities. Healthy hermits is by far the group least preoccupied with activities of daily living. Apparently, they can get around the community and do their shopping, run errands, and fix their own meals.

Responses to Marketing Strategies

Healthy hermits exhibit the most negative orientations toward age-based marketing strategies than any other gerontographic group; they tend to have relatively negative attitudes toward firms and their products.

Age-Targeted. Although a large percentage of healthy hermits (40.3%) are of the opinion that companies should offer more discounts to older than to younger adults, this group's response to senior discounts trails all other older adults in the remaining life stages. Similarly, this group seems to have strong preferences for advertisements that show products especially for older people.

Promotional. Healthy hermits along with frail recluses are the two gerontographic groups least likely to be attracted to special displays in a store, although a large percentage of them (72.9%) indicated they watch the advertisements for announcement of sales. Fewer healthy hermits, frail recluses, and healthy indulgers than ailing outgoers seem to watch ads for sales.

New Products. Healthy hermits are very cautious shoppers. Only one in ten indicated they like to try something new every time they are in the store, trailing ailing outgoers and healthy indulgers. When they decide to buy or use a new product, however, healthy hermits are almost as likely as other groups who seek out information.

Satisfaction with Products/Services. Healthy hermits is the group least likely to experience regret with the products they buy, although two-thirds of them expressed discontent. This group is also more likely to indicate difficulty with opening packages and containers than ailing outgoers and frail recluses.

High-Tech Products. Healthy hermits seem to have a relatively positive attitude toward high-tech products. Only 1 in 5 (21.1%) were of the opinion that high-tech gadgets are too confusing to deal with, suggesting that the remaining older adults in this group expressed either positive or neutral attitude toward high-tech—much higher than older respondents in other life stages. Although healthy hermits is the group most favorably disposed toward these products, they (along with frail recluses) are less likely than the remaining groups to express the opinion that older people should learn to use electronic gadgets and services that can make their life easier.

Payment Systems. Three in four healthy hermits, a number somewhat below the norm for those 55 and over, like to pay cash for most things they buy. Only one in ten (9.0%) indicated they seldom pay off the entire balance on their monthly statement of their charge accounts, the lowest percentage of all gerontographic groups, suggesting older consumers in this group have a high incidence of payment of their charge accounts in full.

AILING OUTGOERS

Demographics

Age. Ailing outgoers are somewhat younger than most older adults age 55 and older. Slightly over half (55.03%) are between the ages of 55 and 65, and only a small percentage (8.79%) are 75 or older.

Sex. Women are somewhat overrepresented among ailing outgoers. In the study whose results are shown in Table B.1, 62.5% of are ailing outgoers are women, a figure that is a few percentage points higher than the norm of 60% for all people age 55 and over.

Living Arrangements. Ailing outgoers are as likely to live with others as the average person age 55 and over. Seventy-seven percent of them report living with at least one other family member or with individuals other than family members.

Education. One of the distinctive characteristics of ailing outgoers is their low level of education relative to older adults in other gerontographic groups. Only about one in five reports having a college education, a figure much lower than that of healthy indulgers (35.11%).

Marital Status. Another distinctive characteristic of ailing outgoers is their relative low likelihood of being married. Nearly three-fourths (74.33%) of ailing outgoers are married; they, along with healthy hermits, are the groups least likely to be married.

Retirement. Unlike most other gerontographic groups, ailing outgoers tend to still be employed. About 36% reported they were retired in our study, a figure much lower than the norm (55%) for the 55-and-over population.

Income. Perhaps the most distinctive characteristic of ailing outgoers is their low level of household income. Although most of them are still working, the vast majority (nearly four in five) report annual incomes below $40,000, a much higher figure than those of older adults in other gerontographic groups.

Location. As with healthy hermits, ailing outgoers are not concentrated in any particular geographic region of the country. However, they are slightly inclined to live in the South, with nearly one in ten of them reporting a southern state as their permanent residence; and they are somewhat more likely than older adults in other groups to prefer urban over rural locations.

Mass Media Use. About half of ailing outgoers spend 3.5 hours daily with the television on, a figure second highest to that of frail recluses. This group listens to the radio more than any other gerontographic group; ailing outgoers also tend to read magazines more than other groups, while their newspaper readership frequency resembles the norm for all older adults age 55 and over.

Needs

Ailing outgoers is the gerontographic group most likely to have a variety of consumption-related needs and concerns. This segment of the 55-plus population scored higher on all measures of needs examined. Obviously, this group is preoccupied with a variety of topics that affect their day-to-day living.

Money. Ailing outgoers is by far the group most likely to be concerned with financial matters. More than half (55.56%) of them are concerned with being able to keep up with bills and weekly expenses, and nearly three-fourths (73.51%) of them expressed concern with remaining financially independent.

Health/Well-Being. More than half (52.81%) of ailing outgoers, the most of any gerontographic group, are concerned with being able to contact someone in case of emergency. Similarly, they are the group most likely to express concern with being mugged, raped, or robbed, with 56.22% of older people in this life-stage segment expressing concern with such crimes.

Social/Family. Ailing outgoers contains the highest percentage of older adults who are concerned with care-giving responsibilities toward their parents, with 21.73% of them expressing concern. One in three of them, also the highest of all gerontographic groups, feels that no one cares for them.

Home. Home-related matters are also of greatest concern to this group. More than three in five (61.27%) of ailing outgoers expressed concern with having their home or apartment burned or burglarized, and nearly one in three (32.04%) were concerned with finding someone to do home or appliance repairs.

Information. Ailing outgoers are heavy consumers of information, with 54.52% of individuals in this group expressing concern with getting useful information on things that affect them, second only to healthy indulgers (60.23%). This group is about as likely as healthy indulgers to demand professional advice on financial, tax, and legal matters, with nearly half (48.46%) of the individuals in this life stage expressing concern with getting useful information.

Leisure. Ailing outgoers and healthy indulgers are the two gerontographic groups most likely to be concerned with finding ways to indulge themselves; and they are considerably more likely than older adults in other life stages to attend special events or activities, with 22.83% of them expressing concern with their ability to attend.

Daily Activities. More than half (51.62%) of ailing outgoers, considerably more than other gerontographic groups, are concerned with their ability to go shopping and run errands. Approximately two in five of the older adults in this group expressed concern with their ability to fix their own meals.

Responses to Marketing Strategies

Unlike healthy hermits, ailing outgoers appear to be the gerontographic group most likely to respond favorably to marketing offerings and strategies of the firm, in comparison to older adults in other life-stage groups.

Age-Targeted. Nearly two-thirds (65.9%) of ailing outgoers, the highest of all groups, expressed the opinion that companies should offer more discounts to older than to younger people. Also, ailing outgoers is the group most likely to say they like advertisements that display products designed for older people, with 36.7% of them expressing preference for such ads.

Promotional. Ailing outgoers are favorably oriented toward promotional strategies. Nearly four in ten (38.9%) admitted they are attracted to special displays in a store (a figure very close to the highest among all groups), and eight in ten indicated they watch the advertisements for announcement of sales (more than any other gerontographic group).

New Products. Ailing outgoers along with healthy indulgers are the two groups most likely to admit they try something new every time they are in the store. The former group is also the group most likely to indicate they use product information, with four in five of older Americans in this life-stage group indicating they attend to information on products before buying or using them.

Product/Service Satisfaction. Although ailing outgoers are favorably disposed toward marketing offerings, they are not always happy with the products they buy. They, along with healthy indulgers, are the groups most likely to indicate they change their minds after buying a product, with 82.6% of them admitting to making buying mistakes. Nearly two-thirds (67.2%) of ailing outgoers, the second highest percentage among the four gerontographic groups, admit that they often find packages and containers difficult to open.

High-Tech Products. Ailing outgoers have a somewhat positive attitude toward high-tech products, more so than two other gerontographic groups. They, along with healthy indulgers, are of the opinion that older people should learn to use electronic gadgets and services that can make their life easier, with 76.8% of people in this life-stage segment expressing such an opinion.

Payment Systems. No other gerontographic group prefers to pay cash for products and services they buy more than ailing outgoers, who gave a very positive response (85.8%) to this method of payment. Interestingly, mature people in this group are also more likely than the average 55-plus consumer to indicate they seldom pay off the entire balance on their monthly statements of their charge accounts, suggesting that although they prefer cash, they often must use credit to finance purchases.

FRAIL RECLUSES

Demographics

Age. Older adults in the "frail recluses" group tend to be somewhat older than the average person age 55 and over, with a little over half of the frail recluses falling in the "65-plus" age bracket. This figure is slightly higher than that for healthy hermits and much higher in comparison to the remaining gerontographic groups.

Sex. The "frail recluses" group contains a disproportionately high number of older men. While about 40% of older Americans age 55 and over are men, 45% of individuals who comprise this group are men.

Living Arrangements. Frail recluses are the second group (after healthy indulgers) to report that they live with others. About 80% of older Americans in this group report living with others.

Education. Frail recluses are among those with the lowest level of education; they have the second lowest education level after ailing outgoers. One in four frail recluses reports having a college education.

Marital Status. Older adults in this group tend to be married; they are the second highest group with married people after healthy indulgers. A little over 80% of older adults in this group report they are married.

Retirement. Perhaps the most unique characteristic of this group is the high number of retirees. While the national norm (percentage figure) for retirees age 55 and over is 55, 70% of frail recluses are retired.

Income. Frail recluses' income is very close to the average for people age 55 and over. Nearly three in ten (28.31%) report total annual household income in excess of $40,000. Although this figure is far below those for healthy hermits and healthy indulgers, it is substantially higher than the income of ailing outgoers.

Location. Frail recluses are less likely than older adults in other gerontographic groups to live in the East. Instead, older adults in this life-stage group are more likely to live in northcentral states than other groups; and they also show a high concentration in southern states. Since this group is not likely to be mobile, its high concentration in those states (northcentral) that have a high outflow of younger people, as well as in states (southern) that have low outflow of younger people may explain these percentage figures.

Mass Media Use. Frail recluses are the heaviest users of television, with nearly 60% of them reporting viewership of 3.5 hours or more daily. They are also the group most likely to report heavy newspaper readership, but they are as likely as the average person age 55 and older to listen to the radio and read magazines.

Needs

While healthy hermits and ailing outgoers are groups with a rather clear pattern of consumption-related needs and concerns, frail recluses are a gerontographic group with very diverse needs. They are concerned with some matters more than the average older person, and with other matters much less than the average older American; and with other matters they are as concerned as the average older consumer.

Money. Frail recluses represent the norm with respect to their concerns with money, with 31.45% of individuals in this life-stage group expressing concern with their ability to keep up with bills and weekly expenses. Being financially independent is also a great concern among older adults in this group. Frail recluses are far less concerned with financial independence than ailing outgoers and healthy indulgers, but much more concerned with this area than healthy hermits.

Health/Well-Being. Although personal safety is in the minds of many frail recluses, individuals in this group are not as much concerned with this issue as individuals in other gerontographic groups. Three in ten (29.07%) expressed concern with their ability to contact someone in case of emergency, and nearly half of them (49.71%) expressed concern with crime such as rape and robbery.

Social/Family. Frail recluses are not the group most likely to expressed concern with caring for their aged parents, with only one in eleven expressing such a concern. However, a significant proportion of them (24.74%) experience the feeling that no one cares for them.

Home. Home-related matters are important in the lives of frail recluses. Nearly half of them (48.65%) are concerned with fire and burglary of their home. One in four in this group also expressed concern with finding someone to do home or appliance repairs.

Information. Frail recluses are generally on the lower end of information use, but much more likely to use information than healthy hermits. A little over one-third of them is concerned with getting useful information on things that affect them, and more specifically information on financial, tax, and legal matters.

Leisure. Frail recluses, along with healthy hermits, are not very concerned with indulging themselves. Only a small percentage of them (3.49%) are concerned with finding ways to enjoy themselves (like travel and entertainment) and nearly as many (4.02%) with being able to attend special events or activities.

Daily Activities. Although frail recluses are somewhat concerned with activities of daily living, they are not as concerned as ailing outgoers and healthy indulgers. One in four expressed concern with their ability to do their shopping and run errands, and fewer than 20% (18.35%) with their ability to fix their own meals.

Responses to Marketing Strategies

Frail recluses' responses to marketing strategies are very diverse; they are favorable toward certain marketing stimuli and not so favorable toward other strategies.

Age-Targeted. Frail recluses are more likely than the average older adult to have the opinion that companies should offer more discounts to older than to younger adults. However, their preferences for advertisements that show products especially for older people are fairly similar to those of an average person age 55 and over.

Promotional. Frail recluses are not as attracted to special store displays as older adults in other life-stage segments, with one-third of them (32.4%) admitting their attraction to such stimuli. Nor do they watch the advertisements for announcement of sales as much as older adults in the remaining gerontographic groups, although seven in ten of frail recluses actually do.

New Products. Frail recluses is the group least likely to respond to new products. They are less likely to look for something new when they go to the store than older Americans in other life-stage segments. Similarly, this group is less likely than other gerontographic groups to try to learn as much as they can about a new product or service before buying or using it.

Product/Service Satisfaction. Although product discontent among older adults is very high, frail recluses are not as likely as older adults in some other gerontographic groups to admit making unwise purchasing decisions. However, this group is more likely than other groups to have difficulty opening packages and containers.

High-Tech Products. Frail recluses are not likely to be prone to new technology, in comparison to other older adults in different life-stage segments. More than one in three (36.5%) find electronic gadgets too confusing to deal with, despite their positive orientation toward older persons' use of such products (65.5%).

Payment Systems. Frail recluses is the second group most likely to prefer cash as method of payment, with nearly four in five expressing preference. Their payment habits regarding charge accounts resemble those of the average older adults.

HEALTHY INDULGERS

Demographics

Age. Healthy indulgers along with healthy hermits are the youngest gerontographic groups, with 54.53% of the older adults in this group found in the 55-to-64 age bracket, and about 9% being 75 or older.

Sex. One of the most noticeable characteristics of this group is its high representation by females. This group contains 10% more females than one would expect to find in the typical 55-plus group.

Living Arrangements. Another distinctive characteristic of people in this life-stage group is the high proportion of them who live with others. Healthy indulgers are more likely to live with someone else than people in other gerontographic groups, with 82.24% of them reporting this type of living arrangement.

Education. Healthy indulgers are more likely than the average person age 55 and over to have a college education. Thirty-five percent of them report having a college education, the highest percentage figure among the four groups.

Marital Status. One of the unique characteristics that stands out among healthy indulgers is the high percentage of them who are married (83.91%). This figure is substantially higher than that for the average person age 55 and over; it is almost 10% higher than the figure for ailing outgoers.

Retirement. Healthy indulgers are likely to still be working, with only 30% of them reporting retirement. This figure is nearly half of what one expects to see for the entire 55-plus population, and certainly is much lower than the percentages for healthy hermits and frail recluses.

Income. Healthy indulgers are relatively well-off financially; along with healthy hermits they report the highest annual household income figures. Specifically, 37.31% report $40,000 or higher total household income.

Location. Healthy indulgers tend to be concentrated in eastern states, where they outnumber frail recluses 2 to 1. They are also likely to live in western states, where they outnumber frail recluses 4 to 3.

Mass Media Use. Healthy indulgers spend less time watching TV than older adults in other gerontographic groups. However, their use of other forms of mass media is very close to the average for the 55-plus population.

Needs

Healthy indulgers have diverse consumption-related concerns, as the data in Table B.2 suggest. Compared to other groups, they are more concerned with certain consumption-related matters but less concerned with others.

Money. Healthy indulgers' concerns with money issues are somewhat diverse. While their concerns with daily bills and weekly expenses represent those people 55 and over, they tend to be relatively more concerned with maintaining their financial independence.

Healthy/Well-Being. Healthy indulgers are about as likely as frail recluses, but much less likely than ailing outgoers, to be concerned with contacting someone in case of emergency. However, healthy indulgers are much less likely than ailing outgoers and frail recluses to express concern with being mugged, raped, or robbed.

Social/Family. Healthy indulgers trail only one group (ailing outgoers) when it comes to assessing their care-giving responsibilities toward their aging parents. However, they appear to feel less isolated than the average older person, and about as isolated as healthy hermits, with about one in six expressing concern that no one cares for them.

Home. Home-related matters of security and upkeep do not preoccupy healthy indulgers as much as other groups. Only three in ten (half as many ailing outgoers) expressed concern with having their home/apartment burned or burglarized. Their concern with finding someone to do appliance or home repairs is low, almost as low as that of healthy hermits.

Information. Healthy indulgers are heavy consumers of information. They are more likely to be concerned with finding useful information on things that affect them, with two in three older adults in this group expressing concern. Healthy indulgers are as likely as ailing outgoers to be concerned with getting good financial, tax, or legal advice.

Leisure. As their name suggests, healthy indulgers are very much oriented toward leisure activities. They, along with ailing outgoers, are far more concerned with finding ways to enjoy themselves than the remaining gerontographic groups. However, the group trails ailing outgoers with respect to concerns with their ability to attend special events and activities.

Daily Activities. When it comes to expressing concerns with activities of daily living, healthy indulgers represent the norm for the 55-plus population. One-third of them, a figure that ranks them the second group behind ailing outgoers, is concerned with their ability to do their shopping and run errands. One in four is concerned with fixing their own meals.

Responses to Marketing Strategies

Healthy indulgers is a very diverse group of older consumers. While they respond positively to some marketing stimuli, they are negatively disposed toward other marketing offerings.

Age-Targeted. Healthy indulgers' responses to age-targeted marketing practices represent the norm for the 55-plus population. Half of them are of the opinion that companies should offer more discounts to older than to younger adults, and about one in four (26.84%) like advertisements that show products especially for older people.

Promotional. Healthy indulgers respond very favorably to certain promotional stimuli and not so favorably to others. Our survey findings show that people at this life stage are those most likely to admit they are attracted to special store displays, with 42.5% of them reporting such a response. However, healthy indulgers along with frail recluses are least likely to watch the advertisements for announcement of sales, even though seven in ten actually do so.

New Products. Healthy indulgers do respond rather positively to new products. Along with ailing outgoers, they are more likely to admit they like to try something new every time they are in the store, with 15% of them reporting innovative behavior. They also report a relatively high use of new product information; nearly eight in ten (77.2%) agree that they try to learn about new products or services before buying or using them.

Product/Service Satisfaction. Although healthy indulgers are generally more dissatisfied with many products they buy than the average older consumer, they are not necessarily dissatisfied with all product features. For example, although 83.5% of healthy indulgers indicated they sometimes wish they could get their money back for something they had bought, the highest percentage among all gerontographic groups, they are not necessarily the group that finds packages and containers difficult to open.

High-Tech Products. Healthy indulgers are generally not as favorably disposed toward high-tech products. Thirty-six percent of older adults in this group admitted in our survey that electronic products are usually too confusing to bother with. However, this group reported the most favorable attitude toward the other older adults' use of electronic gadgets and services that can make their life easier, with nearly eight in ten (77.9%) expressing this opinion.

Payment Systems. Healthy indulgers are the heaviest users of credit, since they represent the group with the lowest incidence of responses to cash as a method of payment (69.3%). This is also confirmed by examining their credit card bill-paying habits. Healthy indulgers along with ailing outgoers are the groups most likely to indicate they seldom pay off the entire balance on their monthly statement of their charge accounts.

SUMMARY OF PROFILES OF LIFE-STAGE GROUPS

The preceding information helps us profile each one of the four life-stage or gerontographic groups on the basis of demographic characteristic, consumption-related needs, and their responses to marketing strategies of the firm.

With respect to demographic characteristics, healthy hermits tend to be somewhat older. The largest percentage of them are retired, and they tend to live in single-head households in relation to their counterparts in other groups. Healthy hermits have higher incomes than the average working older adult age 55 and over. They are also well-educated and have no particular preference for geographic location. Ailing outgoers tend to be somewhat younger, female, with lower education and income than older adults in the remaining gerontographic groups. They are heavy radio listeners and magazine readers. Frail recluses are somewhat older and are likely to live with others. The large majority of them are retired, and they have relatively low income and education. Frail recluses are heavily concentrated in northcentral states, and are heavy users of television and newspapers. Finally, healthy indulgers are relatively younger, predominantly female, married, but still working. They have high education and income; and they make low use of television.

There are several significant differences in older adults' consumption-related needs across gerontographic groupings. Healthy hermits have the fewest needs and concerns. Ailing outgoers are primarily concerned with financial matters, and they desire to maintain their financial independence; they are concerned with health matters and the protection of their home and other assets. Frail recluses are more security-conscious than older adults in other life stages; their concerns with security are confined to physical and home safety, with a very strong desire for physical protection. Finally, healthy indulgers have a strong need for selective information on matters that affect them; they are likely to pursue leisure activities and be involved in volunteerism and other community activities.

Finally, there are some significant differences in responses to marketing strategies given by older adults in the four life-stage segments. The four groups respond rather differently to various marketing stimuli that represent various types of marketing activities of the firm. Healthy hermits tend to be the least responsive to marketing strategies based on age; they have positive attitudes toward technologies for older people and they respond favorably to new technologies, although they are one of the groups least likely to favor technologies designed specifically for older people. Healthy hermits are relatively more likely than other gerontographic groups to pay off the entire balance on their charge accounts and to have difficulty sticking to a savings plan. On the other hand, ailing outgoers are a prime market for consumer products and services, responding very favorably to products and promotional strategies for "older people." Frail recluses report a low use of product information prior to purchase and product use, and difficulty in opening packages and containers. Finally, healthy indulgers have favorable attitudes toward technology; they are attracted to in-store displays more than any other gerontographic group; and they are the group most likely to use credit when buying products and services.

Selected Bibliography

Bartos, Rena. (1980). "Over 49: The Invisible Consumer Market." *Harvard Business Review*, 58 (January-February): 140–148.

Dychtwald, Ken, and Joe Flower. (1989). *Age Wave*. New York: St. Martin's.

Menchin, Robert S. (1991). *The Mature Market: A Gold Mine of Ideas for Tapping the 50+ Market*. Chicago, IL: Probus Publishing Company.

Moschis, George P. (1987). *Consumer Socialization: A Life-Cycle Perspective*. Boston: Lexington Books.

————. (1991). "Marketing to Older Adults." *Journal of Consumer Marketing*, 8(4) (Fall): 33–41.

————. (1992a). "Gerontographics." *Journal of Services Marketing*, 6(3) (Summer): 17–26.

————. (1992b). *Marketing to Older Consumers*. Westport, CT: Quorum Books.

————. (1993). "How They Are Acting Their Age." *Marketing Management*, 2(2): 39–50.

————. (1994). *Marketing Strategies for the Mature Market*. Westport, CT: Quorum Books.

Novak, Thomas P., and Bruce MacEvoy. (1990). "On Comparing Alternative Segmentation Schemes: The List of Values (LOV) and Values and Lifestyles (VALS)." *Journal of Consumer Research*, 7 (June): 105–109.

Ostroff, Jeff. (1989). *Successful Marketing to the 50+ Consumer*. Englewood Cliffs, NJ: Prentice-Hall.

Schewe, Charles, and Anne L. Balazs. (1992). "Role Transitions in Older Adults." *Psychology and Marketing*, 9 (March-April): 85–99.

Wolfe, David B. (1990). *Serving the Ageless Market: Strategies for Selling to the Fifty-Plus Market*. New York: McGraw-Hill.

Index

About the Author

GEORGE P. MOSCHIS is Professor of Marketing and Director of the Center for Mature Consumer Studies, Georgia State University, and a member of the Gerontology Program faculty. An internationally recognized authority on marketing to older adults, he has been a consultant to corporations and government agencies throughout the United States and abroad. He contributes frequently to various consumer and trade publications and is author of more than 100 peer-reviewed articles and papers. His two most recent books, *Marketing to Older Consumers* (1992) and *Marketing Strategies for the Mature Market* (1994), were both published by Quorum, and selected by *Choice* as being among the outstanding academic books of their years.

ISBN 1-56720-062-1

HARDCOVER BAR CODE